Felix Dennis is a poet, a publisher and a planter of trees. Having left home at 15, he found himself living as a poverty-stricken musician in a London bedsit. Without a penny of capital and lacking any business experience whatsoever, he created a publishing and digital media empire which today operates on four continents.

For many years the *Sunday Times Rich List* has ranked him in the Top 100 of Britain's wealthiest individuals.

He is the author of numerous books, including the international bestseller *How to Get Rich,* and has also written five books of highly-praised verse, all of which are still in print. His poetry has been performed by the Royal Shakespeare Company on both sides of the Atlantic. His sixth book of verse, *Tales From The Woods,* will be published by Ebury Press in 2010.

Other interests include commissioning bronze sculpture, breeding rare pigs (and occasionally eating them), drinking French wine, collecting first edition books and avoiding business meetings. His greatest ambition is to complete the planting of a large native broadleaf forest in the heart of England.

He has homes in Soho, Stratford-upon-Avon, Manhattan, Connecticut and the Caribbean island of Mustique.

His website address is www.felixdennis.com.

HOW TO MAKE
MONEY

THE 88 STEPS TO GET RICH
AND FIND SUCCESS

FELIX
DENNI$

Vermilion
LONDON

First published as *88 The Narrow Road*
Published in 2010 by Vermilion, an imprint of Ebury Publishing
A Random House Group company

This edition published in 2011

The Random House Group Limited Reg. No. 954009

Addresses for companies within the Random House Group can be found at

www.randomhouse.co.uk

A CIP catalogue record for this book is available from the British Library

Designed and set by seagulls.net

Excerpt from 'The Hollow Men' from Collected Poems 1909-1962
by T.S. Eliot © The Estate of T.S. Eliot and reproduced by permission
of Faber and Faber Ltd. Excerpt from 'Come to the Edge' by
Christopher Logue © Christopher Logue, 1969,
reproduced with kind permission.

ISBN 9780091935542

Copies are available at special rates for bulk orders. Contact the sales
development team on 020 7840 8487 for more information.

To buy books by your favourite authors and register for offers, visit

www.randomhouse.co.uk

Penguin Random House is committed to a sustainable future for
our business, our readers and our planet. This book is made from
Forest Stewardship Council® certified paper.

Printed and bound in Great Britain by Clays Ltd, Elcograf S.p.A.

For
Dick Pountain
and the Bunch Books gang
at Goodge Street,
where it all
began

We were clappy-happy, we were hippy-dippy—
We were building Eden by the mighty Mississippi.

CONTENTS

FOREWORD

Those who tread the narrow road
Walk in single file–
Shadows plague each wary step,
Hazard haunts each mile.

When I first wrote about the getting of money some
years ago in *How to Get Rich* (a deliberately crass title
whose irony escaped all but a few reviewers), I was aiming to
reach a wide audience. In this, at least, I succeeded; Internet
search engines list thousands of references to the various
editions of that book.

How to Get Rich was designed as an *anti*-self-help manual,
written to dissuade the majority of readers from making
the attempt to acquire real wealth. My book, then, partially
failed in its purpose. Too many critics and readers found it
'inspirational'.

In short, it sold many copies for the wrong reasons, just as
my publishers rightly calculated it might (or so I now suspect)
when they commissioned me to write it. There is nothing
intrinsically wrong with such an outcome. Publishers need to
eat and writers write to be read. Even so, a palliative is in order.

How to Make Money is the result. A shorter book, designed as a tool rather than as an armchair diversion, it turns its back on that vast army who vaguely *wish* to be rich; those who have nurtured an industry by confusing *reading* with *doing*. Instead, these pages offer a brief guide for those determined to attempt the getting of money and willing to shoulder the consequences. Should you not be so resolved, I suggest you discard *How to Make Money* and choose one of the hundreds of other books written (often by charlatans) especially for you.

Certain passages from *How to Get Rich* are included in the pages that follow, but all such extracts have been rewritten and edited for the sake of brevity and clarity. Each principle I am familiar with on the subject is discussed in *How to Make Money*, but it needs to be said that we are engaged in shadow work here, delving where others (perhaps wisely) fear to tread.

As T.S. Eliot once put it:

> *Between the idea*
> *And the reality*
> *Between the motion*
> *And the act*
> *Falls the shadow.*

1
ON MOTIVE

It is a commonplace that men and women are driven to act by inherited genes and upbringing, by 'nature' and 'nurture', or rather, by a combination of the two. The getting of money is no exception to this rule of thumb.

Those seeking wealth must weave such imaginary forces into whole cloth, even while knowing them to be nothing more than the shadow of the past cast upon the present. All such cloth should be dyed and patterned by one's ability, intelligence and determination to succeed, regulated only by conflicting desires and by one's degree of respect for authority or fear of retribution – divine or otherwise.

In short, the tyranny of nature and nurture, so widely believed in by those around us, is a phantom and a delusion. At the very least, it is so imperfectly understood that it can lend itself all too readily to the provision of excuses for inaction.

And why should we care, knowing this to be the case?

Whoever seeks to be rich *must* care. Hidden motives rear their heads constantly and inconveniently. Understanding those motives mutes their ability to restrict our actions and subdue our desires and ambitions.

In the getting of money, then, it is wise to consider one's motives for the getting itself; not necessarily to repent of such

1

desires or to laugh at them secretly (although the latter is no bad thing) but to lay such ghosts to rest in the light of day lest they return later to haunt us in times of difficulty.

Your motives are your own, but to proceed without a clear and honest understanding of them is to invite disaster at a crucial moment. Motive makes a fine horse when tamed by understanding and bridled by wisdom. But matters can go ill later in the day when a wild mare flicks you from her back in the midst of a battle.

The search for wealth has been accounted in many societies an ignoble objective – and perhaps it is. Yet surely it is better to wrestle with motive early and consider its strength at leisure than to be surprised by it at some perilous moment in the future when all is in the balance?

2

ON EXCUSES

The three valid reasons for not attempting to become rich are: (1) I do not wish to be rich; (2) I would like to be rich but I have other priorities; and (3) I am too stupid to make the attempt.

The first reason is Teflon-coated and defies challenge – but one wonders just how many who use it would turn down a surprise inheritance of, say, £10 million?

As for the second, what kind of a world would this be if Vincent Van Gogh had never painted, if Beethoven had had no time to compose, if Emily Dickinson had failed to write a poem? All three died relatively poor or flat broke. Nor have I ever read that the giants of thought and philosophy fared much better.

The third reason is a conundrum. Those smart enough to know they are none too bright might stand a better chance on the narrow* road than they imagine. The rich lists of the world contain a fair number of successful but stupid entrepreneurs.

---

* Why 'narrow'? Because so few people ever tread it and most walk single file. The most talked about road in the world, but the least travelled.

Apart from those listed above, some of which are debatable, there are no other valid reasons why you should not get rich.

In truth, most of the so-called 'reasons' for not pursuing wealth are not reasons at all; they are *excuses*. Pitiful *alibis, half truths* and self-serving *evasions* you have erected to spare yourself from the quiet terror of taking your own financial destiny in your hands and making your dreams concrete reality.

They are the children of fear and the parents of a thousand 'if onlys'.

3

ON WHO IS LIKELY
TO SUCCEED

Anyone in good health and of reasonable intelligence, provided they utterly commit themselves to the journey, can succeed on the narrow road. The commitment is vital. Its component parts are discussed later in this book.

Tunnel vision helps. Being a bit of a shit helps. A thick skin helps. Stamina is crucial, as is the capacity to work so hard that your best friends mock you, your lovers despair and your rivals and acquaintances watch furtively from the sidelines, half in awe and half in contempt.

Self-confidence helps, but can be simulated or acquired along the way. Tenacity is an absolute requirement. Luck helps – but only if you do not waste time seeking it. The belief that you have a great idea is not worth cuckoo-spit. Ideas are ten a penny while the ability to execute counts for a great deal more.

The answer to 'Who is likely to succeed?', perhaps then, is this: not those who *want* to and not those who *need* to or those who *deserve* to, but those who are utterly *determined* to, whatever the cost to themselves and to those around them.

4

ON THE STATISTICAL ODDS

Only 0.000016 per cent of 60 million UK citizens are rich and less than one per cent of one per cent of the population are even comfortably off. If wealth were decided by lottery, you would have 16 chances in a million of scraping into the top thousand richest people in the UK.

Fortunately, wealth is decided less and less by the lottery of inheritance. Only a quarter of the entries in the *Sunday Times* Rich List in Britain are there today due to inherited wealth. Thirty years ago, inherited wealth accounted for three-quarters of the list.

There are factors likely to exclude some from becoming rich. Health is one. People in poor health find it difficult to muster the stamina required to grow rich. We must also factor in disadvantage. Not of sex, race, religion or lack of education – no such 'disadvantages' present insuperable hurdles in a Western democracy – but mental handicap or the onset of senility virtually rule out serious accumulation of wealth.

Close to 40 per cent of people in the UK, then, are either too ill or too old to have any hope of becoming rich or are too young to be able to do so at this time. If you fall into neither of these groups, you now have only 35,999,000 people to overtake.

However, a substantial proportion of the population have no desire to become rich or have chosen professions that rule out that possibility. For example, over five million people work for the government in the UK, directly or indirectly, and are thus unlikely ever to become rich. Your odds have therefore improved to 28 chances in a million.

Now look around you. How many of those you work or socialise with, do you feel might dedicate themselves to becoming wealthy? Two per cent? Three per cent? Five per cent? Let's say three per cent, which I would argue is a gross overestimate. That three per cent of the 30-odd million still in the reckoning amounts to under a million rivals. To reach the top thousand earners, we have shortened the statistical odds to one chance in 900 for you to succeed in the getting of real money.

Finally, should you be willing to settle for a place within the 'comfortably off' rather than, say, the 'lesser rich', your chances of success improve to something like one in 90. (There are approximately 300,000 millionaires in Britain today.)

These odds may still appear daunting, but if they serve to discourage you from the attempt to improve your lot, then you deserve to stay relatively poor. Or, to put it more kindly, whether you *deserve* to or not, you almost certainly *will* stay poor.

5

ON THE REAL ODDS

Providing you live in a country with some claim to being governed by the rule of law; are of reasonable intelligence and in good mental and physical health; and are not presently incarcerated in a prison or an institution, then nothing, absolutely nothing, can stop you from becoming rich.

This is not a wild claim. It is based on close observation and experience.

There is no magic bullet and no secret formula. The issue revolves around only two questions:

- To what degree are you prepared to dedicate yourself to the task?
- How many times are you willing to fail, perhaps publicly and humiliatingly, before you succeed?

In a sense, they are the same question.

While there are qualities that may assist one to succeed more quickly in becoming rich from a standing start – discipline, confidence, self-belief, flexibility, being lucky, a thick hide, the ability to focus, the knack of learning to listen and learning *from* listening, an early inclination to delegate and to motivate those around you – nothing can compete with tenacity. Tenacity will eventually trump all other qualities, whether inherited, acquired or mimicked.

Anyone prepared to dedicate themselves and persevere in the getting of money will eventually succeed.

To such a person, the odds of success are meaningless.

6

ON GETTING STARTED

There is no point in sitting around thinking about getting started – not just for the getting of money but for just about anything.

If you have not made up your mind already, promise yourself you will do so as soon as you have finished reading this book. Better still, this page. Better still, do it right this minute – this 'unforgiving minute'.

Are you going to commit yourself to becoming rich by following the narrow road? Well – *are* you?

Commit now, or leave such dreams behind.

Begin now, or turn away.

6

ON GETTING STARTED

7

ON CHOOSING THE RIGHT MOUNTAIN

The world is full of money. Some of that money has your name on it. All you have to do is dig it out of the mine – but which mine?

Certain industries are more glamorous than others. Some require huge investment, some can be conquered out of a garage. Some are growing, others are in decline. Should you choose only to operate in a glamorous, growing industry? Where is the most opportunity to be found? How do you choose the right mountain?

Forget glamour if the getting of money is your priority. Few of those who wish to start their own movie company or own the coolest PR outfit in the world or steal Steve Jobs's gadget thunder will ever succeed. The reason is obvious. The laws of supply and demand apply not only to commodities but to the choices people make. Too many people wish to make blockbuster movies and live in Beverly Hills. Not enough people wish to start a landfill company and dig holes.

Gold rushes rarely happen in old mines. New or rapidly developing sectors often provide more opportunities to get rich. The reasons for this include: (1) availability of risk capital; (2) investor ignorance and greed; (3) the power of a rising tide.

Investors gravitate to emerging industries in the hope of making a killing. To get rich, you need capital and to acquire it you may need to be where loose capital is searching for a home. Next, the combination of ignorance, greed and misconception surrounding new markets or technologies works in your favour, which is why many investors lost money in the dot-com bubble, and later, to hedge fund bandits.

Finally, the power of a rising tide masks many start-up difficulties, putting newer companies on a more even footing with larger, more established operators, at least for a while. A rising tide floats all boats.

As a postscript, I would add that individual sectors within an industry can make a difference. A small fish in a growing pond is more attractive to purchasers (and to late investors) than the same size fish in a diminishing pond.

8

ON CUTTING LOOSE

You have to cut loose to get rich. There isn't any other way. Cut loose from parents and family, obviously. Loose from working for others, except as a short-term reconnaissance expedition and in order to raise a fraction of the capital you will eventually require. And loose from negative influences – those naysayers and Jeremiahs who cover the face of the earth.

These wretches will tell you, if you listen, of the impossibility – and the foolishness – of trying to make yourself richer than they are. In doing so, they can drain confidence and optimism from you. Surprisingly, such people may include your family, your lover, your husband or wife, or your friends.

It's not that they do not care about you; they may well do. But two fears confront them: they (openly) fear you are placing yourself in harm's way, which cannot be a good thing; and they (secretly) fear that should you succeed, you will expose their own timidity. Above all, they do not wish to be faced with the messy chaos that accompanies strenuous effort and risk. They yearn for the familiarity and sense of false security conjured by the status quo.

This is why you must cut loose. Getting rich comes from an attitude of mind. It isn't going to happen if things drift on pretty much the way they are right now.

9

ON POLE POSITIONS

Young, Penniless and Inexperienced?

Excellent. You stand by far the best chance of becoming as rich as you please. You possess an advantage neither education nor upbringing, nor even money can buy – having almost nothing, you have nothing to lose.

Nearly all great entrepreneurial fortunes were made because, like you, those entrepreneurs had little to lose. In addition, you have stamina, no track record to defend and the single most priceless asset imaginable. What is it? The time necessary to succeed, of course!

Slightly Better Off and On The Way Up?

You've thought about it by now. But you hesitate. Your desire to attempt it is almost outweighed by your fear of losing what you have already achieved. Yet what is fear but the little death: death by a thousand cuts? And how great is the risk, anyway?

You have the experience and the remnants of youthful stamina. *Now* is the time to decide whether you wish to continue to make your employer even richer or, instead, become rich yourself. You are getting too comfortable. It is time to choose.

Veteran Manager or Experienced Professional?

Hmmm. Are you reading this book for vicarious pleasure? Are you experiencing a midlife crisis? Or do you truly intend to make serious money at last? If the latter, you have left it perilously late, my friend.

Find yourself a young and fearless partner. Choose him or her with care. It's your best, perhaps your only, chance to survive and succeed on the narrow road.

10

ON HUMILIATION

Chance comes to everyone in life, often on the most unexpected occasions, radiating risk and potential humiliation.

Those prepared to stop what they are doing, analyse the risk, act in deadly earnest and bear potential humiliation – these are the 'lucky' ones who, when the music stops, will find themselves holding a potful of money.

Anyone can stop what they are doing. A far smaller number develop the ability to analyse risk. Still fewer are prepared to act in deadly earnest for as long as it takes. And only a minute fraction are prepared to bear the humiliation of being made to look a fool.

If you have ever wondered why there are so few really wealthy self-made men and women in the world, you now have the answer. It has little to do with chance and everything to do with your capacity to accept the risk of being humiliated in the attempt – not just once, but many times, perhaps.

11

ON COMMON IMPEDIMENTS

- If you are unwilling to fail, sometimes publicly, and even catastrophically, you will never be rich.
- If you care what the neighbours think, you will never be rich.
- If you cannot bear the thought of causing worry and concern to your family while you walk in the shadow of the narrow road, you will never be rich.
- If you stay too long working for others, you will never be rich.
- If you have artistic inclinations and fear the search for wealth will coarsen your talents or degrade them, you will never be rich. (Because your fear, in this instance, is justified.)
- If you are not prepared to work longer hours than anyone you know, you will never be rich.
- If you cannot convince yourself that you are 'good enough' to be rich, you will never be rich.
- If you cannot treat your quest to get rich as a game – a silly game with serious rules – you will never be rich.

12

ON THE TIGER CHAINED
TO YOUR ANKLE

What is the first question asked by strangers of each other? It's 'What do you do?'

In some cultures, the way of answering may be different; but nearly always relates to work: 'I'm a teacher; I'm in banking; I'm a dairy farmer; I'm an administrator; I'm a sound engineer.' Our job defines us.

But it cannot define you. Not any more. You are a wild pig rooting for truffles. You are a weasel about to rip the throat out of a rabbit. You are an entrepreneur. You are going to be rich, and you don't much care, within the law, how you are going to do it. Or what must be sacrificed in the attempt.

You will do anything it takes, short of larceny, fraud, blackmail and murder. You may have cut yourself loose, but the tiger chained to your ankle has come right along with you. He will always be with you, until the day you turn him loose by an effort of will. The day you leave the narrow road to riches.

Until then, he requires pretty regular feeding. His name is Ambition. You can call him 'Ambo', if you like – but it won't make his teeth any less sharp.

You have changed in order to be free to make a whopping great fortune while your tiger scares the hell out of little old ladies and rivals. And yourself, for that matter. All self-made men and women are fettered to such a companion, whether they choose to acknowledge his existence or not.

If you do not have a tiger handy as you read these words, I suggest you acquire one soon if you wish to amass serious wealth. Without him, all the tenacity in the world will avail you nothing.

13

ON FRUGALITY

Equipping a new company costs a small fortune. I wince every time I enter the premises of start-up companies and spy stunning reception areas. Overspending on such accoutrements is rife in start-ups – it is as if the owners require the false reassurance of unearned ostentation.

A beautiful vase of flowers in reception every week creates a better impression than £100,000 worth of fancy Italian furniture. Office furniture need not be bought new – why not purchase it from the last fool who set out to reassure themselves they had it made before they earned a penny? All computers and similar kit should be leased. In the early days, everything possible should be leased or outsourced. Start-up capital is simply too precious to squander on physical purchases.

The creating of a frugal company culture begins on the first day. Staff travel and entertainment should be checked with an eagle eye – including your own. Issuing staff credit cards or company cell phones before the company can afford them is just showing off. Company cars will transport you down the road to ruin. Air travel on any class but economy is preposterous. Leaving lights, printers, computers, copiers and the like on 'stand-by' overnight is plain stupid.

Even if your new company breaks even or makes a profit in its first year (a dubious proposition) it is likely that your profit margin will be tiny – in the 10 per cent range, say. Thus you will have to generate revenues of ten times the money spent on what might have been avoided to equalise your cash position.

Revenues are not within your control. Cash spent on perks and kit is. Multiply each pound you had thought to spend on such items by ten times *before* you approve their purchase. Your appetite for them will be sensibly diminished.

14

ON COMMON
START-UP ERRORS I:
MISTAKING DESIRE
FOR COMPULSION

Most people wish to be rich. But wishes are feeble, ephemeral things and whoever wastes too much time in the 'hissing laboratory of his wishes', as the poet Dylan Thomas once put it, is doomed to failure.

Compulsion trumps desire in two ways: intensity and longevity. Those who feel compelled are more likely to focus relentlessly and exclusively on the attainment of a particular goal. In addition, they are likely to shrug off repeated failure and return to the fray with undiluted energy.

Those who merely *desire* to achieve something, and then attempt it, risk not just failing, they risk undermining their self-belief. The road to riches is a marathon, not a sprint. While it may fleetingly boost one's ego to line up at the start of a race with bona fide marathon runners, the consequences of exhaustion and collapse can be catastrophic when the inevitable occurs.

Life is not a rehearsal. The getting of money may be a silly game, but it is a game with serious rules. It requires a level of discipline and toleration of hardship which is inimical to what most people regard as the purpose of a fulfilled life. Only the participant's absolute certainty that the goal can be achieved makes such a marathon tolerable.

Do not mistake desire for compulsion. Only *you* can hear the song of your inner demons. Only *you* can know if you are willing to tread the narrow, lonely road to riches. No one else can know; no one else can advise you. Nor do they have the *right* to advise you. When the going gets tough, when all seems lost, when partners and luck desert you, when bankruptcy and failure are staring you in the face, all that can sustain you is the fierce compulsion to succeed *at any cost*.

Inner compulsion is mandatory in the getting of money. Either you have it or you do not. Wishing you had it is no substitute.

15

ON COMMON
START-UP ERRORS II:
FAILURE TO MONITOR
CASHFLOW

Cashflow is the lifeblood of any business. Failure to moni-tor cashflow is the source of most start-up failures.

Regular, obsessive monitoring is the key. This is a tedious chore for entrepreneurs because few are born bookkeepers, but cash is vital to any enterprise – far too vital to be left to accountants. Cashflow is the heartbeat of a company. An understanding of its importance is essential before you set out. If the heart stops, the body dies. Lack of cash dooms an enter-prise to bankruptcy, or, just as surely, leads to others prising control from its founder.

Once control of a business is lost by running out of cash, you will be relegated to the status of minority investor or salaried employee, or tossed on to the scrapheap. No one will care how bright the future is for the company you created. No one will listen to your entreaties. Having lost control due to poor management of your company's cash, no bank, white knight or new investor will permit you to regain control. Why should they? You failed once and may fail them in turn.

If cashflow is good, then no matter how badly run or poorly managed a company might be, there is always a chance of turning its fortunes around. At the very least, there is *time* enough to do so. But if cashflow is poor, panic sets in and events spiral swiftly out of control.

The root causes of cashflow going awry are many. Perhaps the business is not viable, or has expanded too quickly. Under-capitalisation is a frequent culprit. As is the 'ostrich syndrome', where inexperienced managers or owners focus only on new business while neglecting mundane tasks like meeting payroll or tax demands. Are overheads too high? Has bad debt crept up to unacceptable levels?

Obsessive monitoring and forecasting of cash levels cannot, of themselves, generate cash. But they *can* provide a start-up's owner with an early warning – one that may well make the difference between ruin and survival.

16

ON COMMON
START-UP ERRORS III:
EXCESSIVE OVERHEAD

There is never a time in a company's history when cost control can be relegated to the back burner, but for a start-up company, keeping costs low is a vital necessity. One golden rule is: '*Overhead walks on two legs.*'

Overhead will eat you alive if not constantly viewed as a parasite to be exterminated. Never mind the bleating of those you employ. Hold out until mutiny is imminent before employing even a single additional member of staff. More start-ups are wrecked by overstaffing than from any other cause, bar failure to monitor cashflow.

Consider this: to pay a member of staff may cost, say, £20,000 or so. To *obtain* that £20,000 in order to squander it on payroll, most companies would have to generate revenues between £100,000 and £200,000 (assuming a profit margin of 10 to 20 per cent) just to stand still. After factoring in other costs associated with hiring that member of staff, revenues would have to rise by £135,000 to £235,000. Even if such new revenues *are* forthcoming, the company will be no better off that year.

Always ask yourself this question: is this hire *really* necessary? So necessary that I feel certain that employing this person will enable us to generate *additional* income amounting to seven to ten times the new employee's base salary?

Overhead grows by osmosis. By doing nothing to attack, control and reduce it, an owner risks waking one day to discover that the rats of overhead in the deepest holds of the ship have multiplied to the point where they have gnawn through the crew's provisions – or even the ship itself.

17

ON COMMON
START-UP ERRORS IV:
REINFORCING FAILURE

Reinforcing failure is perhaps the most difficult error to avoid in business.

There are two possible causes. The first is the difficulty of establishing whether one *has* a failure on one's hands. The second, when a failure is clear, is linked to an inflated belief in a project's potential or to a reluctance to publicly admit failure – or both.

How costly can reinforcing failure be? Very. Empires have been lost in messianic reinforcement of failure. Compare the collapse of the USSR with the rise of China: the first continued to reinforce the failure of its state-owned industries; the second quietly instigated a U-turn on the ground. Today, the USSR no longer exists while China is ranked third in world GDP.

Some failures are a matter of timing. What used to fail, now succeeds (cut-price airlines). What once was a sure thing, no longer works (land-based telephone systems). Unfortunately, start-up companies do not enjoy the luxury of time. They may withstand the failure of a particular project, but they cannot withstand the cost of sustaining and reinforcing that failure until circumstances change.

How to avoid this trap? Firstly, do not fall in love with any project. You may believe in it wholeheartedly, but must remain prepared to abandon it should it show signs of failing. (Slow-burn successes are few and far between.) Secondly, examine whether the failure lies in the product or service itself or in its implementation. Does nobody want it, or have you hired the wrong team to produce or sell it?

You imperil all you have worked for by putting off the day of reckoning. Reinforcing failure is not investing in the future. Turn your back on heroics – they have little place in the getting of money.

18

ON COMMON
START-UP ERRORS V:
SKIMPING ON TALENT

If you are determined to become rich, there is only one talent you require: the talent to identify, hire and nurture others with talent. Any company managed and run by plodders and jobsworths will be lucky to survive, let alone prosper. Talent is the key to sustained growth, and growth is the key to early wealth. You cannot afford to skimp on it.

To ensure that a talented individual will work for you, or will *stay* working for you, be flexible. Money is not always the great motivator here. Talent knows its value, of course, but surprisingly often is more attracted to new opportunities and challenges. The currency of that value is not necessarily a million-dollar salary. The chance to prove itself, or the opportunity to run the show on a day-to-day basis, may do the trick just as well. What talent seeks, as often as not, is the opportunity to excel.

Youth is a further factor. Young talent can be found and underpaid for a short period, providing the work is challenging enough. Then it will be paid at the market rate. Finally, it will reach a stage where it is being paid on past reputation alone. And that is when you must part company with it.

Anybody wishing to become rich cannot do so without talent, either their own or the talent of others. Talent is indispensable, although it is *always* replaceable. There are six simple rules concerning talent: identify it, hire it, nurture it, reward it, protect it from being poached. And, when the time comes, fire it.

If you can do these things with talent in the context of building your company, I would be truly astonished if you did not become rich. Talent does most of the work for you, just as it has done since the beginning of recorded history. After all, who created the Egyptian pyramids? The pharaohs or the engineers?

Think about it, then go hire the best talent you can find – just as the pharaohs did.

19

ON BOLDNESS

Whatever you can do, or dream you can, begin *it—*
Boldness has genius, power and magic in it.
Johann Wolfgang von Goethe

The most successful generals and admirals in history shared one characteristic: they were willing to disregard orders and risk disgrace in order to exploit rapidly changing circumstances. When the chance came, they recognised an opportunity, weighed the odds swiftly and placed their lives and careers on the line to snatch a victory.

In short, they were bold, often turning a blind eye (quite literally in Nelson's case) to previously agreed strategy while ignoring direct instructions from their superiors. As an entrepreneur you are unlikely to have to follow the orders of others, but the fetters of conventional wisdom can prove equally inhibiting.

Fortune favours not just the brave but the *bold*. Boldness has a kind of genius in it as Goethe points out. It relies on the unexpected and can lead to catastrophic defeat because it ignores conventional wisdom, which often proves to be wisdom of a kind. But should boldness succeed, the resulting success appears all the more devastating in the eyes of startled observers and rivals.

Opportunities to get rich keep popping up. The more alert one is, the more chance one has of identifying an opportunity; the more preparation one has done, the more artillery one can bring to bear; the more self-belief one can muster, the more certain will be the aim; but the *bolder* the stroke, the better chance one has of confounding the odds.

All entrepreneurs have a short- or medium-term game plan; it's the only sensible way to proceed in the getting of money. But should the chance offer itself, that game plan must be hurled aside and the watchword on the narrow road changed to: *'Carpe diem!'*

20

ON BEING IN THE RIGHT PLACE AT THE RIGHT TIME

You are reading the wrong book. It is always the right time and this is the only place we have.

21

ON RICHES AND HAPPINESS

Other than in the first flush of acquisition, wealth cannot confer happiness. To the contrary, it is certain to impose a degree of disharmony and irritation, if not from the stresses and strains involved in obtaining and protecting it, then from the guilt that inevitably accompanies its arrival.

Wealth is preferable to poverty, but not conducive to contentment. This dichotomy has always been with us. The philosopher Lao Tzu speaks for the defence in the *Tao Te Ching*: 'Be content with what you have; rejoice in the way things are. When you realise there is nothing lacking, the whole world belongs to you.' But the poet Alexander Pope, arguing for the prosecution two thousand years later, remained unconvinced:

Get place and wealth, if possible, with grace;
If not, by any means get wealth and place.

The rich are not a contented tribe. The demands from others to share their wealth become so tiresome, so insistent, they often decide they must insulate themselves. Insulation eventually breeds a mild form of paranoia.

And what of trust, of camaraderie? The only people the self-made rich can trust are those they knew *before* they became wealthy. As with the onset of sudden celebrity, for the newly rich, the world often becomes a darker, narrower, less generous place; a paradox which elicits scant sympathy, but is nonetheless true.

There are consolations in the acquisition of wealth, but they do not (and cannot) include contentment. Somewhere in the invisible heart of all entrepreneurs is a sliver of razored ice, the whetstone of ambition. Without you release it, you will fail. Contentment is its sheath. Once released, the sliver will grow – that is its nature – but the sheath will wither.

Thus you must choose between seeking riches or seeking contentment. You may achieve neither, but you surely cannot seek both.

22

ON WORKING
FOR OTHERS

For those determined to succeed in the getting of money, earning a living working for others can prove useful. But beware! Given time, a salary begins to exert an attraction and addictiveness all of its own; regular payslips and crack cocaine have that in common. More to the point, working too long for others will serve to blunt your appetite for risk. And in risk lies the only sure path to riches.

You will never get rich working for your boss.

You are not looking for a 'career', except as a launch pad or a chance to infiltrate and understand a particular industry. Such employment should provide excellent training for the struggle ahead and will act as a salutary reminder of the fate of the vast majority of wage slaves condemned to work for others until they retire.

Sounds pretty arrogant and selfish, doesn't it? Not exactly 'playing the game' or exhibiting what a human resources manager would call 'constructive team attitude'. But then, who ever heard of a rich human resources manager?

In reality, you are *not* part of a team, although you may have to pretend otherwise in order to better understand how companies function. You should certainly do so conscientiously. But in your secret heart, however hard you work, you must not deceive *yourself*. Working for others is a reconnaissance expedition; a means, not an end; an apprenticeship, not a goal. And learning to dissemble convincingly is a useful (though not essential) skill on the narrow road.

While working for others, promotion is welcome and brings with it the chance to learn more; but your primary purpose for being there is to suck out the marrow of what you need to know – to understand it and place it within a greater context for a future goal.

The goal of getting rich.

23

ON RAISING CAPITAL I: SOURCES OF CAPITAL

Western capitalism may be a rotten, debased system of managing human affairs, but it is the only system to have survived the demise of all its rivals. Nor is it called capitalism for nothing. For any hope of success, an individual must acquire capital, or at least access to capital. Moreover, this must be done in such a way so as not to prejudice a final and favourable outcome.

There are only six ways of obtaining capital. You can be given or inherit it; you can win it; you can steal it; you can marry it; you can earn it; you can borrow it.

Inheritance rarely leads to the establishment of any worthwhile business enterprise. It breeds a sense of privilege and complacency, for the most part. There are, of course, exceptions to this rule, but fewer than should be statistically probable.

'Winning' capital is perhaps the riskiest of all undertakings. Even for those at near-genius levels, gambling is a time-consuming, precarious and totally exhausting occupation. As for mass games of chance, surely the only sensible view is that the 'lottery' is merely a pleasant name for organised racketeering.

The rewards of theft (especially so-called white-collar fraud) can be high, but who would wish to wake each morning wondering if this is the day you will be handcuffed and marched off in front of startled workmates or neighbours, bound for a nasty, dangerous environment – possibly for years?

As to marrying wealth, this has a nice ring to it, but rich in-laws often know very well – better than your innocent spouse, in fact – just why you married. Jealous spouses, too, often become expert at extracting their pound of flesh, while the outside world's attitude to gold-diggers of either sex invariably interferes with the creation of a successful business. To be blunt, who wishes to be sneered at by colleagues and peers for years to come?

We are left, then, with two options: either earning capital or borrowing it.

24

ON RAISING CAPITAL II:
EARNING IT

Earning money to use as capital to create a new business is a sure strategy, but carries a penalty – a penalty measured in time. It might well take 15 to 25 years to accumulate sufficient capital to start a new business of one's own.

For most who have worked for others for so long, the stamina and risk-taking attributes of youth have usually fled. The clattering dream is still alive, perhaps, but the driver is semiconscious. And there is a further, less obvious drawback to earning capital. A decent salary is addictive; one eventually becomes dependent upon it.

It takes a brave man or woman in such a position to launch into the maelstrom of a start-up.

In addition, one is rarely permitted to hone the skills required by entrepreneurs while working for others. Risk-taking by senior staff is frowned upon in most large organisations, unless one happens to work in the money markets for a financial institution.

Certainly it can be done, but the success rate of those who take the plunge into personal-wealth generation in middle age is depressingly low. At best, money made working for others can provide *seed* capital. Such seed capital is not to be despised, however. Those who lend money to entrepreneurs are often encouraged by the level of commitment demonstrated by the risking of an applicant's seed capital.

Few, then, earn sufficient capital to launch out on their own without borrowing, either from banks or from others. Even should they do so, the likelihood is that they will turn away from risking all they've worked for on a reckless dream when push comes to shove. And on the narrow road, pushing – and shoving – is an occupational hazard!

25

ON RAISING CAPITAL III: AVOIDANCE OF FAUSTIAN PACTS

All Faustian pacts in the raising of start-up capital should be avoided. The surrender of a controlling stake in a business by an entrepreneur in exchange for working capital, or a war chest to expand, is always a dubious proposition. No matter what promises are made at the time of the exchange, such loss of control will inevitably give rise to negative (and even dire) consequences. A founder can be removed from the business. The direction of the business can be arbitrarily altered by the majority shareholders, probably in search of short-term gain at the expense of long-term asset value. Or worse, in search of precipitate growth.

No founder of a business who surrenders control in exchange for capital is ever likely to retrieve control of that business. Their financial destiny is in the hands of others and the entrepreneur has lost their way on the narrow road.

The terms upon which capital is raised are crucial to the long-term goals of any entrepreneur dedicated to the getting of money. It is one of the few decisions that can change the course of one's life.

26

ON RAISING CAPITAL IV: SHARKS

The world is awash with money. But there are predators to beware of in this sea of potential capital. Sharks are one.

Those intent on the getting of money must avoid sharks like the plague. I shall not insult your intelligence by warning against the ruinous usury of loan sharks. Anyone who has borne the burden of a loan that sucks the lifeblood from you week after week, leaving you exhausted and no further forward than when you started, will tell you what a terrible price such borrowing extracts from the human spirit. Better to labour as a wage slave than as a cash cow for a loan shark.

Their 'respectable' cousins can be every bit as dangerous. Perhaps you have read stories about people who launch a small company by taking out a dozen credit cards and juggling cash limits for a few months to obtain capital? While they make for exciting reading, such tales nearly always end tragically.

If such loans are not paid back swiftly, the most promising acquisition or start-up will likely fail. While the venture itself may have real merit, the mountain of debt from such loans rapidly becomes the focus for whoever is running the business – and a business that loses focus on its products or customers, *for whatever reason*, is in peril. In addition, your personal credit rating is extremely precious and difficult to repair. It really is imperative to avoid a history of credit default.

The interest rates charged by all species of sharks are beyond the capacity of any legal business to sustain. While bankruptcy laws have become more generous to creditors in recent years, a history of bankruptcy will plague and hinder you when you seek to return to the fray.

Forget sharks. There are far better, albeit onerous, methods of raising capital.

27

ON RAISING CAPITAL V:
THE NATURE OF DOLPHINS

Venture capital organisations are sometimes referred to as 'dolphins', a nickname deriving from their frantic desire to 'flip' every deal as quickly as possible. The best of the dolphins boast a ton of managerial talent and experience. They tend to know what they are talking about in the abstract, if not in your particular niche.

Dolphins care little about the eventual destiny of any business they invest in, but the return of their investment, together with a massive bonus for the risk they took and the skill they provided, is mandatory. This, in turn, leads many of them to move from an advisory to an operational (and dominant) role in any business in which they invest. Indeed, they are notorious in this regard. To them, growth is a god in its own right. The medium- and long-term future of the business is not their concern, for the obvious reason that they do not intend to be shareholders for very long.

Venture capitalists will do anything it takes to protect their investment in your business. They are protecting their most priceless asset – their reputation.

Venture capitalist short-termism, its eye firmly glued to the sale of an enterprise within three or four years, is the hallmark of nearly all venture capital activity. As is their insistence on a massive stake (often a controlling one) in those businesses for which they provide capital. Experience has taught them that this control is the course most likely to return the profits required to satisfy their *own* investors, the great fleas on *their* back. In the glorious lines of Jonathan Swift:

> *So, naturalists observe, a flea*
> *Hath smaller fleas that on him prey;*
> *And these have smaller fleas to bite 'em,*
> *And so proceed* ad infinitum.

Dolphins are not an evil bunch; far from it. They are mostly smart, well-connected, persuasive, and passionate about success. But their first loyalty is to the quick buck rather than to any start-up they invest in – least of all to a start-up's founder.

28

ON RAISING CAPITAL VI:
PLAYING WITH DOLPHINS

Venture capitalists, dolphins, being what they are, just what are the perils of approaching them or encouraging their advances in order to grow or to cash out? Plenty.

Firstly, they can be hard to convince. Having done so many deals in the past, they are the least starry-eyed tribe you will ever encounter. Secondly, the price they will demand is that you hand over a chunk of equity before they invest. Thirdly, many insist on a date by which your company must be sold, either back to yourself or to others. Fourthly, should you not meet certain monetary targets along the way, they may steam in and take control of what you have created.

Time and again I have watched existing companies wishing to expand, or new ventures anxious to get started, mire themselves with the slippery dolphins. A few succeed, and succeed gloriously, it has to be said. But a great many other original owners or founders are squeezed out long before the fabled 'big pay day'.

Venture capital money, dolphin money, is not for the faint-hearted. Too often, it is only for the desperate or inexperienced, unless building a business for a quick(ish) return and a small piece of the action is your goal. And there is nothing wrong with such a goal in the short term.

The dolphins are consummate professionals – to them you are just another amateur in the sea trying to stay afloat, to grow, to make your financial dreams come true. Amateurs are easy meat. But it will not be the dolphin's corpse spiralling down into the depths if things go wrong. He will live to fight another day.

You, on the other hand, will be shark bait.

29
ON RAISING CAPITAL VII: BANKS

Banks are an odd lot. And the word 'bank' covers a great deal of ground, much of it quite useless to a start-up entrepreneur.

I taxed a senior British banker with what he looks for when considering whether to loan money to a serious start-up entrepreneur. Here is his response:

- The principal (that's you!) must have a lot to lose in the venture.
- A history of previous failures is a red flag. (One failure is fine.)
- Going up against serious competition without deep pockets is a red flag.
- Is the idea a good one – not unique (red flag), but with strong potential?
- Does the principal appear determined, a hard worker, frugal, steady?
- Is there an experienced partner, investor or mentor somewhere in the picture?

- Much depends on the point in the economic cycle when the request is made.

Banks, then, are willing to help; but only those who help themselves. They are not a rich uncle or your fairy godmother. If you have failed to raise some capital yourself, then, frankly speaking, there is little point in approaching them.

Most commercial bank loans have to be cleared by a 'credit committee'; the banker you are speaking to is probably not in a position to make the decision unilaterally. It goes without saying that your business plan must be clear and accurate, and must contain no wild assumptions concerning revenue generation.

When negotiating bank loans, treat expensive 'arrangement fees', personal liability in the event of default and 'balloon' repayments with caution. It is often better to try to separate loans into short- and medium-term pots, each with a different repayment arrangement. Timely repayments impress bankers, as do regular summaries sent to them demonstrating your company's trading position.

Banks are easier to deal with when you have a history of previous loan repayments. Perhaps their only weakness is a horror of losing valuable custom to a rival bank.

30

ON RAISING CAPITAL VIII: SWIMMING WITH THE FISHES

Swimming with the fishes is the combination approach to raising capital and the most likely way forward. Sharks must be avoided. Banks help only those who help themselves and dolphins will pay you no mind at this stage. But the fishes are all around you. You are one yourself.

- Save seed capital while working for others. If expenditure is cut to the bone, you may be able to save up to 50 per cent of what you take home after taxes. This requires discipline and sacrifice, but is entirely within your own control.
- Create a sensible, modest plan with no wild assumptions to show to other fishes. Seek help from someone accustomed to business plans to assist you.
- Relatives and friends are a good source of start-up capital. Such money is best taken as a loan (not in exchange for shares if you can avoid it); staged repayment dates, with interest, should be agreed in writing.

- If you have a rich, older relative, ask if they are considering including you in their will. This is cheeky, but if they will *loan* or *give* you a part of what they intended to leave you – with or without repayment – so much the better.
- Suppliers are canny fishes, only to be approached when you have some capital in the bank. If your product is to be sold via a distributor, the distributor may be prepared to promise to pay a supplier before your company receives a penny. This helps avoid advance payments to suppliers. It's a long shot, but I've known it to work.
- Introductions to suppliers and sources of capital from those experienced in any business are invaluable. Treat such introductions with respect and reverence. In such circumstances, it is better to appear overly deferential than too familiar.

Raising capital is an odious task. But look at it this way. Those who dream of becoming rich but will not abase themselves to do it will become your employees. *They* will remain wage slaves. *You* are going to become rich.

31

ON RAISING CAPITAL IX: 51% INVESTORS

Again, you are reading the wrong book. Very, very few entrepreneurs who accept a 51 per cent partner in a new venture will get rich if they are also expected to run it. Control is mandatory.

It is better to plot and plan to raise sufficient capital to start a business where you call the shots, no matter how long it takes. If an investor will accept 51 per cent of all dividends or bonuses or distributions made from the company while leaving you with 51 per cent of the voting stock – fine. (Providing there is an exit strategy built into the arrangement.)

It's the control that counts. Period.

32

ON CREATING THE
RIGHT ENVIRONMENT

You cannot get rich all on your own. No one can. You
have to work within (or, more likely, create) the right
environment.

Humans are cooperative, if argumentative. If you were to
be boycotted by others, if nobody would meet with you or
take your instructions or sell you anything or buy anything
from you, you could never make money. You just can't do it
on your own.

Getting rich is mostly sleight of hand. If you acquire
no audience but a mirror there is no illusion with which to
get rich.

Take a common fantasy, the 'James Bond' scenario where
an evil genius works alone with a computer on the Internet to
steal all the world's money. This evil genius needs someone
to *guard* the gold bars while he works his evil; to *make* him the
computer in the first place; to *invent* the Internet to permit
his evil to spread as well as minions to *pump out* the evil lava-
tory when the evil sewage pipe is blocked.

You see? You just can't do it alone. You need to create an
environment.

This does not mean that you require fancy offices and all the accoutrements. Human capital is by far the most important element of your environment, whether you're starting up or deep in the game.

By focusing on obtaining the right human capital you vastly increase your chances of becoming rich. Your employees, colleagues, professional advisors, suppliers and customers are all human capital. Choosing those that will serve you best is an art form.

33

ON START-UP HIRES

When a company is established, the best people to do the hiring are your managers. It is they who are going to have to ensure their own promotion and bonuses based on the daily performance of these hires. But in the earliest days of a start-up, you will likely have to do the hiring yourself.

What are you looking for with start-up hires?

Stupid people are easy to hire. The world is full of the none-too-bright. Many of them are extremely pleasant to work with, don't cost too much and will give you a lovely smile each morning. But they will not add to your wealth, and in the early days you should shun them like the plague. What you require are clever, cunning and adept people.

Why would clever, cunning and adept people work for you?

The answer is simple; there are many clever, cunning and adept people who are risk-averse. You are *not* risk-averse because you are dedicated to becoming rich. Believe it or not, much cleverer people than yourself will happily work for you, providing they do not have to brave the narrow road. The willingness to hire those cleverer than yourself is a potent weapon in the getting of money.

Choose them with great care. They are the foundation of your future fortune and are as valuable as the start-up capital they devour. They are *human* capital. Success or failure, riches or ruin, dreams or nightmares: everything is encompassed within the skill and enthusiasm of these start-up hires.

34
ON HIRING GENERALLY

- Do you *need* to hire anyone? Will such a hire permit the company to increase revenues by seven to ten times the base salary of a candidate? If the answer is 'probably not', don't make the hire.
- Try not to choose key employees by yourself. Have others interview them and compare notes. This guards against the natural impulse to hire those similar to oneself.
- Don't just rely on a candidate's CV. If you can, speak to their previous employer.
- Be alert for 'crossovers'. Many candidates not quite suited to the job you have on offer at the time may well be suited to a future position.
- Be courteous but formal at interviews. Prepare a list of tough questions to ask. It may appear rude to initiate a conversation and not make small talk, but you are not conducting such interviews for politeness's sake. Say little if the interviewee grinds to a halt – that way, you will learn swiftly how they react under pressure.
- Ignore prejudices, likes and dislikes. This is not only good law, it's good sense. Effectiveness, integrity,

adeptness, professionalism, a desire to shine in the world – these are the attributes you seek. Who you like or do not like is irrelevant.

- Never shoot from the hip with a spontaneous 'You're hired!' *Think it through.*
- If a candidate appeals strongly to you, be prepared to increase your offer. Human capital is the foundation of business success. A thousand here or there is a small price to pay for hiring star talent. One star is worth a dozen plodders.

35

ON MANAGEMENT

In the UK, a Managing Director (MD) is usually in overall charge of a single entity or a group of allied entities. Chairman is an anomalous title, often (within start-ups) the owner of the most voting shares. A Chief Financial Officer (CFO) and Chief Operating Officer (COO) do pretty much what it says on the tin. In a start-up, the roles are often combined and they report to the MD. A Chief Executive Officer (CEO) is a daft title at small start-ups. Save it for later when several entities require individual MDs who need to report to a group chief.

There are two paths once the launch phase is over and it is clear that a start-up will survive. The first involves an owner managing the business. The other is for an owner to take an active chairman's role and release day-to-day control to an MD. Often, an entrepreneur owner will assume the combined duties of MD and chairman for a limited period, then hand over the first of those roles to someone better suited to an MD's role. Most entrepreneurs make lousy managers. It is possible, but not usual, for an owner to take no seat on a start-up's board and hold no executive position. In such a case, the owner is effectively a 'passive investor'.

The crucial element in all this is for an owner to decide the degree of control he or she will exercise over other managers and for those managers to understand and agree precisely where they stand and who will be reporting to who. Clarity is all. There can only be one captain of a ship – that captain is the MD.

As an owner, you have the right to set the destination of the ship, but not the right to give sailing orders once you have appointed an MD. Any ship piloted by two captains will sink. Nor can you, as owner or chairman, fire other senior managers at will – that is an MD's prerogative. You may fire your MD, but may not publicly undermine their authority. Argue, advise, consult and debate all you wish with your captain in private, but you may not *and must not* do so on deck.

A company's fate lies in the hands of its managers. How you manage those managers is as vitally important as training yourself not to *compete* with them. They are not rivals; they are your colleagues and employees and you are mutually dependent upon each other.

36

ON ETERNAL LIEUTENANTS

The world is full of eternal lieutenants – a blessèd tribe to aspiring entrepreneurs.

Such people desire job security, job satisfaction, a degree of status and a sense of belonging far more than they desire wealth. Loyal to a fault, with deep reserves of integrity, they are as hardworking and as punctual as they are polite. Although they may quietly protest otherwise, they have little real ambition. Quite often, they will work with you for decades. They are the salt of the earth.

Seek out these eternal lieutenants as soon as you can afford them. Be sure to know what you are looking for: you require a tireless collie dog, not a poodle. Favourites and poodles breed resentment.

When motivating the salt of the earth, you may discover financial incentives count less than with other employees. What eternal lieutenants crave is *respect*. And that is what they deserve: trust and praise; the ability on your part to discern when a good job has been done and the courtesy to remember to say so; camaraderie.

Eternal lieutenants cannot replace the need for raw talent in a company, but they can ease the burden of workloads in the early days, being readier than most to shoulder more than their fair share of toil. In addition, they help create an atmosphere of calm in the maelstrom of a start-up: the eye in the storm, the oil on the water.

Just never fall into the trap of promoting them beyond their competence. By so doing, you will lose a great middle manager while causing unnecessary heartache. They will blame themselves when they fail – and, trust me, fail they will.

37

ON THE START-UP AND THE LONG WOBBLE

There are three stages in the course of any business: the start-up, the long wobble and the settle-down of continuous revolution. Here, we examine the first two.

In the heady days of start-up, a degree of risk-taking is a vital requirement for all concerned, as is the capacity for shouldering huge amounts of work. Corners will be (and must be) cut. Nimbleness of mind, flexibility in work patterns and a messianic belief in the project are key. You are creating a pirate ship, not an oil tanker.

During the long wobble, other skills within your work force come to the fore. Better knowledge of rival products or services; closer attention to profit; the consolidation of departmental responsibilities; the introduction of professional managers. And, sadly, the weeding out of personnel no longer suited to such an enterprise. In short, the long wobble reflects a period of painful change to a slightly less entrepreneurial culture. None of this should imply overstaffing or empire-building.

The long wobble is a dangerous time. Initial fires of passion have cooled a little. There will be grumbling from ambitious staffers (often the most valuable talent in the company) and effort must be expended to placate and moti-vate them to stay. The best of them may consider leaving to launch their own start-ups. An owner's best course is to judge if they are serious and either attempt to 'turn' them with new projects or responsibilities (or more money) or congratulate them as they leave the building. Make your wishes for their success as sincere as you can.

That way, they will be tempted to return to work for you should they fail. Some will make perfect candidates to inspire and manage the continuous revolution of the next stage.

38

ON THE SETTLE-DOWN AND CONTINUOUS REVOLUTION

In the third stage of a new company's development, the settle-down, owners should consider initiating a new regime – unless they have already decided to sell the business and cash out.

This new regime will be regarded by ensconced professionals with the same horror their own introduction engendered among the original pirate crew. It is time for the reintroduction of youth and talent, with just one or two steely veterans left on board in senior positions. This sudden introduction of less-experienced personnel (a kind of continuous revolution, if you like) is predicated on two assumptions.

The first is that professional managers inevitably acquire a mindset which argues that experience counts for more than the virtues of what they now perceive as youth. In short, they become comfortable and stale. The second assumption is that the world will have changed, along with the technology, services and products required to excite customers. The young are street-wise consumers of what is new and adapt effortlessly to emerging trends.

Promoting the young at the expense of the experienced brings other, less tangible benefits: their stamina, their ability to brush off setbacks and return to the fray, their desire to impress others and to succeed. Lastly, the promotion of these Young Turks will encourage meritocracy and unravel cronyism, at least for a year or two.

While not a strategy for the faint of heart – and not likely to be welcomed by existing management – the repeated third-stage introduction of waves of Young Turks will maximise profits by ensuring a company's sustained performance over decades. After all, there is only one sacred cow in your organisation.

No prizes for guessing who that might be.

39

ON TEAM SPIRIT

Team spirit is for losers, financially speaking. It is the glue that binds losers together – a strategy used by employers to shackle useful employees to their desks.

While lives may depend on team spirit and teamwork in professions like soldiering or firefighting, in commerce it acts as a subtle handicap and brake to ambitious individuals. Which, in a way, is what it's designed to do, as you will undoubtedly discover when your own managers trumpet the mantra of team spirit to those who will work for you in the not too distant future.

The truth is uglier. As the owner, you are in a team of one.

Anyone arguing that this is an old-fashioned, dinosaur-like approach to business is either an academic or a teacher, probably at a fancy business school. They will be full of hot air and exciting theories concerning 'cooperative alliances', 'partnering' and 'new ways' of doing business.

Phooey!

Note that they will never have risked everything *they* own on the narrow road. In truth, they are sometimes ashamed to teach red-in-tooth-and-claw entrepreneurial capitalism to students or are projecting a kind of wish-fulfilment. Such professors may know a great deal about business theory and management techniques.

But they know nothing whatever about the getting of money.

40

ON GLORY HOUNDS
AND TOADS

Should you already have started a company with more than a dozen members of staff on the books, I can virtually guarantee that one of them is either a glory hound or a toad. That person needs firing; and they need firing *now*.

Like all forms of politics, office politics can be fun, but to many people they are upsetting and seriously interfere with productivity. Worse still, if a glory hound or a toad is in a position of authority, they may well cause talented personnel to up sticks and leave. Indeed, such miscreants *want* more talented individuals to leave: their own feeble light will then appear to burn a little brighter.

It is easy during the frantic urgency of a start-up to ignore such foibles. Easy, and wrong. By setting an example early on that you will not countenance any form of bullying, sneering or bossiness, you will create an atmosphere (a culture if you like) of loyalty, efficiency and camaraderie. An atmosphere poisonous to toads.

Experienced leaders will tell you of the importance of morale. It *is* important. Good morale cannot compensate for sloppy work or an ill-conceived business plan, but a pervasive feeling of 'us against the world' in a start-up company, combined with the promise of promotion based on achievement – this can move mountains. And can just as easily be destroyed in a few weeks by glory hounds (who seek to steal praise for the efforts of others) and toads (who sneer at any junior person's honest error).

Glory hounds and toads often interview well. They have to; it's just about their only talent. Be vigilant. If someone whose work you valued resigns or threatens to resign suddenly, be sure to question them in private. You may be surprised by what you learn.

41

ON DECISION BY CONSENSUS

The road to riches begins with commitment and proceeds upon the basis of decisions and actions taken. A committee, on the other hand, formal or informal, is 'a cul-de-sac down which ideas are lured and then quietly strangled'.

In the words of an American wit: 'a committee is a group of the unwilling, chosen from the unfit, to do the unnecessary.' Indeed it is. 'Collective responsibility', so sensible in politics and the boardrooms of large companies, has little place in the thinking of pilgrims on the narrow road.

A founder is in a team of one. Immersion in 'team spirit', 'consensual decisions' and other morale-boosting jamborees – as well as the shuffling of blame later from one part of a group to another should matters go awry – has little part to play. You're on your own. Collegiate, self-congratulatory corporate committees come later, probably soon after you've cashed out.

Why is this? Because, in a start-up, there is so little time for decisions reached by consensus; so little room for manoeuvre; so little money; and so many, many things to go wrong. Later, when matters are more settled, when massive fortunes have been established, there are often revisionist histories fabricated by former tigers who wish to be seen by the world as consensual, do-gooder pussycats.

Good luck to them. But I have arm-wrestled some of those tigers. There was no 'consensus' in them then. No give. They were as merciless in their ambitions as I was in mine.

In the beginning, it is you who must make the important decisions. Listen by all means – listening intently is one of the most underrated of all entrepreneurial talents – but defer to no one. Think of it as a game of poker. Would you trust even your best mate (one with money on the table) to advise you on whether to draw or hold? Of course not. So it is with the getting of money.

And so it has always been.

42

ON PARTNERSHIPS AND MINORITY INVESTORS

The main requirement for partnerships or minority investors must be the exit plan.

It is crazy and irresponsible to enter into the one or accept the other without such a plan in place. Failure to do so can eventually lead to weeks, months or even years of effort spent hammering out a bad-tempered settlement.

The benefits of partnerships and minority investors are obvious: they spread the burden of risk and can make possible what otherwise could not be attempted. Most partnerships are created on the basis of three criteria:

1. Who is investing what capital into the project?
2. Who will be actively working on the project?
3. Who brings what value to the project?

My advice, my earnest advice, is that you should attempt to establish yourself first, retaining as much control of any start-up or acquisition as you can. Then, and only then, feel free to seek pastures new with partners in the picture. That's a great way to spread risk and to expand, especially into a new sector or geographical location, while retaining at least one major asset you know to be yours and yours alone.

Partnerships can be wonderful, but they are not a marriage, except of convenience. Ideally, you should have something of your own to fall back upon should the partnership fail. This eases the stresses and strains all partnerships must endure from time to time.

As to minority investors (I am assuming you would not be so foolish as to attempt to become rich by starting a company as a minority shareholder) they are a burden. And, sometimes, a bloody nuisance. But they are necessary in many cases and must be treated with consideration and fairness at all times.

Then get shot of the blighters just as soon as you sensibly can.

43

ON THE MEXICAN SHOOTOUT

One of the more amusing, and deadly, clauses that can be inserted into any new minority-investor or partnership agreement is the 'Mexican Shootout', a brutal but highly effective mechanism for resolving disputes.

A clause is inserted in the agreement governing serious disputes between partners or investors. If a dispute cannot be resolved, those shareholders who wish to participate consider carefully what they would be willing to pay for the *whole* company. They must have access to the sum they have in mind, less the worth of their own shares valued on an equal basis. An agreed provision is made for the company's own cash.

All parties appoint a neutral lawyer and, on a certain day, bring a sealed envelope containing nothing but the amount they are willing to pay. The lawyer opens the envelopes. Whoever has bid the highest is now the owner of the company and must pay the 'losing' side for their shares based on the 'winning' bid. (In time, the 'winner' may sincerely wish they had been the 'loser', if they bid too much and saddle their company with unrepayable debt in order to gain control.)

The Mexican Shootout is a brilliant, hair-raising solution, and there are umpteen variations on it. But there are drawbacks as well. It rather depends on which side of the fence you find yourself. In general, the shootout favours minority investors.

From the minority shareholder's point of view, it offers the only chance they may ever have to own the entire company. From the majority shareholder's point of view, the shootout offers an opportunity to be rid of a troublesome pest. But the majority shareholder has more to lose.

Shootouts can save months of argument, lost sleep and teeth-grinding negotiations between partners or investors. If I was a *majority* shareholder, I would strive for no shootout. If I was a *minority* investor, I might not invest without it. And if an *equal* partner? Sorry, but that's your problem. Equal partnerships suck!

44

ON HARNESSING
THE FEAR OF FAILURE

Anyone determined to create wealth from a standing start must make a pact with themselves to abandon the fear of failure. One cannot banish fear, but one can face it down, crush it, bury it, padlock it in the deepest recesses of your heart and soul – and leave it there to rot.

Just try. Go on, I dare you! Try for a single day; one whole day when you refuse to acknowledge fear of failure, fear of making yourself look like an idiot, fear of losing your lover, fear of losing your job, fear of falling ill, fear of getting old, fear of any kind. If you can do this, you will transform your life.

Better still, you can *harness* fear. Think of it not as the King Kong of bogeymen, but as a mare. A night-mare. A mare is a horse. A horse can be tamed, bridled, saddled and ridden. Harnessing the power of a creature that has oppressed you for so long will add mightily to your own. Thus the nightmare of prospective failure provides you with the very means to succeed, affording you the opportunity to feed on the adrenaline you will experience when you confront and master it.

Fear of failing in the eyes of the world is the single biggest impediment to amassing wealth. Trust me on this. It will cripple you. You must confront and harness it.

If you shy away, for whatever reason, then the gate to the narrow road is shut.

And it is shut for ever.

45

ON THE FALLACY
OF THE GREAT IDEA

There is a fallacy rooted in the minds of many who wish to become rich – the fallacy of the great idea.

Having a great idea is not enough. It is the manner in which ideas are *executed* that counts. Implementation will always trump ideas, however good those ideas are.

Good ideas are like Nike sports shoes. They may facilitate success for an athlete who possesses them, but on their own they are nothing but an overpriced pair of sneakers. Sports shoes don't win races. Athletes do.

I have lost count of the number of men and women who have approached me with their 'great idea', as if this, in and of itself, was their passport to instant wealth. The idea is *not* a passport. At most, it is means of obtaining one. In some instances, a fixation on a great idea can prove hazardous, distracting your attention from the perils and pitfalls you will inevitably encounter on the narrow road.

If you never have a single great idea in your life, but become skilled in executing the great ideas of others, you can succeed beyond your wildest dreams. They do not have to be your ideas – execution is all. When confronted with a great idea, your reaction should be to scrupulously analyse its commercial potential in the context of your own ability to transform that potential into triumph.

Ideas don't make you rich. The correct execution of ideas does.

46

ON DRESS CODES

Many will argue that dress codes are immaterial in the getting of money. Perhaps they are right. Certainly I have been outsmarted across a negotiating table by those dressed in the most casual way imaginable.

When you are starting up, however, I believe you should dress conservatively in business attire with the traditional accessories. After all, it's *you* asking *others* to invest in you, to work for you, to become suppliers to you, to trust you. By dressing in what some may consider an old-fashioned way, you show respect without exhibiting undue deference.

It is a matter of personal choice, but I have found the habit useful in another way. When I put on my suit, white shirt, tie and black shoes, I am subconsciously donning armour. I am going out to do battle. Nobody will *give* me more money – I am going to have to *earn* it. By dressing in this way, I remind myself I am dressing for war, not stepping out for a stroll in the park.

Do 'clothes make the man'? For many men and women I think they do, although I accept there are those in California and elsewhere who find such attitudes quaint. Good for them. Perhaps the day will come when the business suit will be relegated to museums – but that day is not yet here.

One last thought. You should insist that salespersons working for you dress conservatively. Ignore protestations to the contrary. There are still large numbers of people in business who object to salespeople making calls in casual attire.

The same goes for your senior managers. They are role models to younger staff, whether they like it or not.

47

ON PROMOTING
FROM WITHIN

Promoting from within is not an issue in the early days of a start-up. Later, it will become a burning issue for those who work for you.

A good rule of thumb is that an external candidate for a key position should appear at least 30 per cent better on the surface than an internal candidate. Why? Because you will already be aware of the faults of the latter, such as they are. External candidates, on the other hand, come to you free of known faults. All one is presented with is an impression from an interview, a word, perhaps, from their ex-employer and a list of their achievements. Failings are not a part of anyone's CV.

Internal promotion has many merits. It permits Young Turks to rise. It can galvanise a department or an entire company. It speaks of your commitment to meritocracy (or should do) and brings with it the comfort of the devil you know. It encourages young talent to stick with you.

Such promotion can carry with it the danger of advancing a member of your staff beyond their competence (the old 'Peter Principle'). This is a serious hazard and should be addressed dispassionately. You do no favours to anyone by falling into that trap, despite the quite natural desire of any owner to reward past loyalty and performance. Beware, too, of glory hounds and toads thrusting forward favourites for promotion in order to increase their own power base.

Owners should treat internal promotion with the same importance attached to it by those they employ. While it is sensible to ensure a steady trickle of new blood into an organisation (because small companies easily become introverted), promotion from within is a powerful tool in an entrepreneur's armoury.

Use it wisely – even humbly.

48

ON THE PARADOX
OF OWNERSHIP

Man alone lays claim to ownership. Other animals merely defend their nests, their territories, their young, their pack, their food.

We purport to believe that individuals or groups can 'own' the most astonishing things: islands, mines, mountains, forests, rivers, hills and deserts, even what lies under the ground or beneath the sea – that humans can 'own' real estate where dinosaurs once roamed. What can this have to do with the getting of money?

In a practical sense, nothing; but from a motivational point of view, such a collective delusion illustrates how silly the chasing of wealth really is. It defies logic because we are mortal and can take nothing with us. Wealth may provide *access*, but never true *ownership*. I 'own' thousands of acres of land in England, but those who work and walk that land daily own it in a far more profound way than I ever can, or ever shall.

The getting of money is a *game*. As the author G. K. Chesterton put it: 'To be clever enough to get all that money, one must be stupid enough to want it.' And herein lies an opportunity. While the objective is absurd, the rules are deadly serious – precisely the reverse of the position taken by many who wish to become rich. In their estimation, the objective is serious while the rules are often absurd.

If one chases money in the belief one can never be happy without it, in the serious belief that the chase is a meaningful occupation, I doubt the probability of success. But an appreciation of the absurdity of the task helps – and helps especially when the going gets tough and events are conspiring to overwhelm you.

Contracting an incurable disease is a serious matter; the death of a loved one is a serious matter; even the rejection of your affections can be a serious matter. The making or losing of money is *not* a serious matter.

Those who understand this and act upon that understanding have a far better chance on the narrow road than their neighbour.

49
ON OWNERSHIP

I f ownership in general is a collective human delusion, and we are all little more than consenting thieves, how can we become successful thieves as quickly as possible?

To become rich you must be an *owner*. And you must try to own it all. You must strive with every fibre of your being, while recognising the idiocy of your behaviour, to retain control of as near to 100 per cent of any company you can. That is the dirty, rotten little secret of it all.

To become rich, every single percentage point of anything you own is crucial. It is worth fighting for. It is worth suing for. It is worth shouting and banging on the table for. It is worth begging for and grovelling for. It is worth lying and cheating for. In extremis, it is even worth negotiating for.

Never hand over a *single share* of anything you have acquired or created if you can help it. Not one share, no matter what the reason – not for loyalty, not for fairness, not as an incentive – unless you genuinely have to. (Shares as an incentive rarely work in any case; there are far better ways to motivate employees.)

Nothing counts but what you own in the race to get rich. If you haven't much skill, or much wit, or much talent, or much luck, and yet you insist on owning more than your fair share of any start-up or acquisition, then you can become rich.

If you choose to forget or to ignore everything else in this book, just retain this:

Ownership isn't the most important thing in the getting of money – it is the only thing.

50

ON CUSTOMERS

There is only one boss. The customer.
And he can fire everybody in the company
from the chairman on down,
simply by spending his money somewhere else.
Sam Walton, founder of Wal-Mart Stores, Inc.

Your customers are the final arbiters of your financial destiny. Not that they are infallible. As Henry Ford pointed out, if he'd asked his customers what they wanted before the first Model T rolled off the assembly line, they would have asked him for faster horses that ate less.

Even so, start-up entrepreneurs do not enjoy the luxury of historical context; their product or service needs to sell – and needs to sell pretty damn soon after the launch of the company. There are few slow-burn successes in commerce.

For some start-ups, the consumer is the only customer one needs to consider. For others, there may be two or more customer bases – distributors and retailers among them. (Media and entertainment providers and the like must also factor advertisers and sponsors into their customer mix.) Each customer base must be approached quite differently and the selling proposition crafted accordingly.

Of all the surprises likely to confront start-up entrepreneurs, customer *conservatism* and *inertia* often tops the list. Can't they see that the product or service you are offering is so much better than what exists? Maybe they can, maybe not. Either way, it will take every ounce of charm and persuasion you possess to shift their purchasing habits.

If you are reading this book, I know you have already thought about this. From hard and bitter experience, I urge you to keep thinking and keep researching your future customer base(s). Hone your USP (unique selling proposition) to a razor-sharp instrument. It is so very easy to get the marketing message wrong, no matter how excellent and innovative your product or service.

As another very great retailer once lamented: *'There is no victory over customers.'*

51

ON SUPPLIERS

Good suppliers respect attention to detail and prompt payment.

Do not hesitate to challenge quotes and invoices from suppliers. At the beginning of a relationship, everything will usually be hunky-dory. Later, hidden or unacceptable costs often creep in. Challenge them.

Request frequent quotes from a supplier's rivals; annual reviews are a lazy man's option. Demand compensation if a supplier screws up based on the financial consequences of the screw-up to your company, not on the value of goods or services supplied.

A supplier is not your 'partner', despite the acres of New Age rubbish you might read concerning 'partnership alliances' between suppliers and customers. Getting rich is not about 'partnerships', especially of that nature. This goes double for banks. You will find out just how close a 'partner' you are to your bank the first day you fail to make a repayment. (To add insult to injury, banks can be the worst suppliers known as far as stealth costs are concerned.)

Good suppliers respect a hard-nosed attitude – providing it's logical and you *pay* on time. In return, you will find that suppliers with whom you forge a good relationship are reliable sources of market information. Many successful deals begin with a quiet whisper in your ear from a supplier.

Treat your suppliers with respect while you keep them on their toes. If you find yourself running short of cash, contact them *before* this becomes evident. Quite naturally, suppliers detest being kept in the dark and told only at the last minute that you cannot pay them. By fessing up early, you may turn a potential embarrassment into grudging respect that you behaved more responsibly than other customers.

52

ON NEGOTIATING

In 1625, Britain's answer to Machiavelli published a book, an edition of which has sat beside my bed for the last 30 years – his *Essays*. Here is what he has to say about negotiating:

> *If you would work* [negotiate with] *any man, you must either know his nature and fashions, and so lead him; or his ends, and so persuade him; or his weakness and disadvantages, and so awe him; or those that have interest in him, and so govern him. In dealing with cunning persons, we must ever consider their ends, to interpret their speeches; and it is good to say little to them, and that which they least look for. In all negotiations of difficulty, a man may not look to sow and reap at once; but must prepare business, and so ripen it by degrees.*

Let us be thankful we shall never have to negotiate with Sir Francis Bacon!

Serious negotiations do not include management bargaining with personnel. Each requires different skills and many good managers should be excluded from serious negotiations. (They have too much empathy.) Important points to remember in serious negotiations include:

- Most of us are poor negotiators (including those sitting across the table).
- Most negotiations are unnecessary.
- Detailed preparation is of inestimable value.
- Whoever depends the least upon the outcome will usually prevail.
- Tenacity nearly always trumps eloquence.
- If in doubt, walk out.

As the owner of a growing start-up, do not permit professional advisors or potential purchasers to lure you into interminable discussions and 'negotiations'. They are often little more than fishing expeditions. Lastly, on serious negotiations in general, it is worth engraving Marguerite de Valois's variation on an old Italian proverb into your soul:

It is the same in love as in war; the fortress that parleys is already half taken.

53

ON PRIORITISING

There is only one enemy. Time. Health, wealth, even love and affection can be reclaimed if all goes for the best; time never can. Time wasted can never be recaptured.

Time spent recharging your batteries and maintaining your physical and mental health is *not* wasted. It is a necessity. Time frittered away attending to tasks easily achieved but relatively inessential to your ultimate goal *is* wasted – a criminal waste of a precious resource.

Prioritising is the key – a key never discovered by a surprising number of otherwise resolute entrepreneurs. If you will not prioritise your tasks for the day, the week, the month (even for the year) and execute them on the basis of their relative importance, you remain at the mercy of your idle subconscious and happenstance.

The making of lists of things to do can be helpful, but not if ticking off items on lists in a random manner becomes a habit. It scarcely needs saying that the most difficult or odious tasks are those that require tackling first.

Ruthless prioritising in the getting of money is the sign of a disciplined, determined mind; one far more likely to succeed. The happy-go-lucky may call it an obsession. So what? I doubt you will meet many happy-go-lucky souls on the narrow road.

Prioritise everything in your working day!

54

ON LUCK

No one can pretend that luck and chance do not appear to exist. If one rejects any notion of the supernatural whatever – as an atheist or a humanist with a capital 'H' – then one must also accept that life itself on this planet arrived by luck or by chance. One cannot have it both ways.

So just what can those intent on the getting of money do to improve their luck? The logical answer is nothing. Nothing at all.

The first-century Roman philosopher Seneca coined the only definition that might prove of some practical use: 'Luck is what happens when preparation meets opportunity.' This has morphed over the centuries into cracker-barrel sound bites from celebrities and sportsmen: 'The harder I practised, the luckier I got.'

Preparation is the key. Being prepared to do the heavy lifting and the homework in advance. Getting on with the job in hand, but remaining alert enough to spot a lucky opportunity when it arrives and then hammering at it with prepared intensity. If one is not prepared, the opportunity will go begging. If one is not alert, all the preparation will be for naught.

One thing is certain. Praying for luck in the getting of money is futile. If Lady Luck exists, she is highly perverse, choosing to visit those who have little apparent need of her and ignoring others desperate to worship at her shrine. Perhaps the best thing is to ignore her. In modern parlance, to 'treat her mean to keep her keen'.

Do not rely on her attention or arrival. Single-minded concentration on the task in hand and the overall goal must be the rule, rather than reverently waiting for some propitious moment when all seems set fair for success.

Waiting on Lady Luck is folly and 'if only' the saddest phrase in the language.

55

ON SHORTCUTS

*Y*ou idle wretch!
    You believe, in your folly and your pride, that there are 'shortcuts' to wealth. Oblivious to your own sloth, you seek for a 'magic bullet' to slay the vampires of poverty that suck your blood each night. You are a fool.

    You will curse those who succeed. It was never your fault, was it? Fate was always against you. You searched as hard as you could, yet found no bullet, silver or otherwise, and are now reduced to scavenging the bitter fruit of charity, either from individuals or the state.

    I have seen you in many guises, many places. And now I find you here, in this bookshop, leafing quickly through the preceding pages, looking for yet another 'shortcut', hoping you won't have to buy my book but will be able to extract the marrow of it without cost to yourself. You miserable worm. You will learn nothing and you will never be rich.

    Know this: your path though life will be a torment of wrong turnings and 'shortcuts' to blind alleys, prophesied by poets and philosophers down the ages. Let the great American writer H. L. Mencken provide your epitaph:

The inferior man's reasons for hating knowledge are not hard to discern. He hates it because it is complex – because it puts an unbearable burden upon his meagre capacity for taking in ideas. Thus his search is always for short cuts.

Just so. Now replace this book on the shelf. There are plenty of other books aimed at the idle and credulous like yourself, mostly written by charlatans who promise 'shortcuts' to the getting of money. But this is not one of them!

56

ON COURTESY

Courtesy is not a cardinal virtue in getting rich. For the most part, it's every man and woman for themselves on the narrow road.

Any experienced entrepreneur will tell you stories of legendary self-made bastards who appear to deliberately foster an aura of discourtesy – even fear – around them as a tactic to keep both outsiders and employees on the back foot. The daily strain of meeting after meeting in the cause of filthy lucre can sometimes do that. As can congenital shyness, paradoxically enough.

Being courteous while you continually fail merely makes you a gracious loser. That said, courtesy can grease the wheels where force will not prevail. It lends a certain gravitas and creates the impression of someone you might like to do business with. In that sense, courtesy is a highly effective form of charm.

This is true in any country of the world, but is nowhere more true than in the home of red-in-tooth-and-claw capitalism, the USA. It is impossible to be too polite in the USA. Americans worship courtesy almost as much as they worship money. Almost.

In Asia – Japan especially – excessive courtesy is habitually employed as a subtle form of barbarian-baiting; it should be reciprocated in the same spirit if you do business there. In Mediterranean Europe, I prefer to be thought a frigid, ill-mannered Anglo-Saxon – and thereby reckon to have saved months of my time and perhaps half a million calories from firmly declined lunch invitations.

Courtesy can enhance efficiency. It is discourteous to accept mobile telephone calls while in meetings or to secretly fiddle with your BlackBerry at conferences. People have gathered together to listen, to inform and to be informed, not to be distracted by your thoughtlessness.

Try to be courteous if you can. It will not make you richer in and of itself, but as a form of self-imposed discipline, it can certainly make you appear more formidable.

57

ON DEBT

How much debt is sensible to carry on the narrow road? Profits are ephemeral and can be measured in different ways, but the total annual revenues of a company are cold, hard fact. Revenues rarely fluctuate by more than 10 or 20 per cent annually, while profits can increase or diminish wildly. It may be wise, therefore, to equate debt levels only with revenue, projected or actual.

My own rule is to keep company debt, if at all possible, to less than 25 per cent of annual revenues. In some years, far less. With luck, such debt could be paid off, at a pinch, within a year or 18 months. This level of debt is perfectly manageable in most instances, but would be considered ridiculously low by other entrepreneurs. Much depends on the economic cycle and interest rates.

'Capping' and 'collaring' debt within fixed parameters of interest is an attractive but expensive option. So is dividing debt into short- and medium-term parcels repayable at differing rates. All balloon-type debts (repayment weighted to a huge repayment at the end of a cycle) should be avoided. 'Arrangement fees' by banks are usury and should be fought tooth and nail.

Some corporate appetite for debt has astonished me over

the years. As I write, one publicly traded rival has debts approaching the equivalent of two years of their annual revenues. Holy cow! They will be working for the consortium of banks that made those loans until Kingdom Come.

Failure to repay debt represents the only event – apart from criminal wrongdoing, death or senility – by which an owner can be forced out of a business. Hence my reluctance to accept levels of debt which might have permitted faster growth. Is it not better to own a smaller, profitable company outright than a larger one owned, in reality, by banks or others who have loaned the money to expand it?

58

ON INTELLECTUAL PROPERTY

Intellectual property refers to the ownership of copyrights, trademarks and patents.

Ideas cannot be 'owned' by anyone. You cannot trademark or patent or enjoy copyright in an idea. You can only protect the *execution* of that idea and, perhaps, its look and feel. Later, you may trademark its name or its tag-line description. A patent usually refers to the sole right to make, use or sell an invention or process.

This is often misunderstood by entrepreneurs and inventors who come to others with an idea, perhaps to raise capital. They may believe that they can protect their idea by asking the potential investor to sign an NDA (Non Disclosure Agreement), but most NDAs offer only limited protection in law.

Much copyright occurs automatically. Say you design and distribute a newsletter; your copyright (providing it contains original material) becomes yours without more ado. But *trademarking* a newsletter's name is more time-consuming and expensive. The body of law relating to intellectual property differs from country to country and expert knowledge must always be sought regarding it.

Suppose a member of staff comes up with an idea your company develops which proves to be a success. Who owns it? The answer is that your company does if the employee put forward the idea while working for you – especially if company time and materials were utilised to further its development.

You would be wise to reward the innovator, however. If they have conceived one great idea, why would they bring the next to your attention if you neglect to reward them sufficiently? Instead, you might find yourself with a rival determined to seek retribution – and rightly so!

59

ON EMULATING

There is an often overlooked adjunct to the subject of ideas in commerce; stealing them. Or, to put it more pleasantly, emulating them.

The error of failing to emulate a winning idea pervades every industry, at all levels, and always has done. Often this is due to indolence or folly. Of indolence, no more need be said. The folly, on the other hand, usually takes the form of a peculiar and pernicious affliction, known colloquially as the '*it wasn't invented here*' syndrome. I would place this affliction very high on the list of reasons preventing individuals and companies from achieving major success.

Why managers and owners should be loath to emulate success is puzzling, but even a condensed history of resistance to change in commerce would fill an entire library. The result of such ostrich-like behaviour can be catastrophic and, in retrospect, unintentionally hilarious. Owners of canals attempting to buy land in order to frustrate railway pioneers is a good historical example. What the (very rich) owners of canals *should* have been about was emulating the ideas of the railway builders and stealing their thunder.

On a mundane level, the refusal of organisations to accept that rivals have adopted a better way of doing something, or a better something to do, creates opportunities for entrepreneurs the world over. Those intent on the getting of money should challenge their own personnel to keep a close eye on the activities of all rival organisations and report immediately any development they consider significant.

Emulating success requires vigilance and an examination not only of the template of any new process or product, but the cause and ramifications of its very *raison d'être*. What works for others on the narrow road will very likely work for you, too.

60

ON DELEGATING

All who learn to delegate wisely (and early) increase their chances of success in the getting of money to a significant degree. Micromanagers, by contrast, unwittingly 'kill the thing they love' and endanger their odds of making real money.

The joys and benefits of skilled delegation are numerous, but let us begin by examining a key quote from the philosopher and mathematician Bertrand Russell:

> *Work is of two kinds: first, altering the position of matter at or near the earth's surface relatively to other such matter; second, telling other people to do so. The first kind is unpleasant and ill paid; the second is pleasant and highly paid.*

I would add that the person who employs the person who tells others what to do is even better paid. And always will be. Why? Because telling others what to do is called management and managers rarely become truly rich, while entrepreneurs and founders of businesses often become rich, despite being poor managers.

Entrepreneurs and moguls are often poor managers because they never had time to practise the art of management. They were too busy delegating and becoming rich.

While there are other benefits involved in delegating wisely (feeling virtuous for having promoted talent and industry, for example, or the confidence such a culture imbues in staff), the real reason for the astounding success rate of this strategy is the time it frees up – time that can be used by an entrepreneur to create a second or third business to accelerate and facilitate the getting of money.

There are perils in sloppy delegation. Nor should one confuse delegation with abandonment. Absentee landlords rarely prosper. Skilled delegation does not come easily to some – there is a knack to it that improves with time – but it is one of the most powerful forces at the command of those determined to create personal wealth.

61

ON TRUSTING
YOUR INSTINCTS

Come to the edge.
We might fall.
Come to the edge.
It's too high!
COME TO THE EDGE!
And they came
and he pushed
and they flew...
Christopher Logue, *Come to the Edge*

This is a potentially lethal piece of advice. And yet, for me, it separates the wannabes from the *gonna*bes. Perhaps, in the end, it is the difference between an attentive eternal lieutenant and the pirate captain who comes to own the ship.

You are not attempting to be a manager, or even a businessman. You are concerned with the getting of money. You must go with your gut. After that, the managers and the bean counters and financial advisors can take over. But only *afterward*.

Trust your instincts. Avoid being a slave to them, but when those instincts are screaming *Go! Go! Go!* it is time for you to decide whether you *really* wish to be rich or not. You cannot do this in a deliberate, considered manner. You cannot get rich painting by numbers. You can achieve it only as a lone predator: by out-waiting rivals; by remaining alert, constantly sniffing the air; by bringing murderous force to bear upon your prey.

And to do so (say it softly!) without consulting anyone or anything but the secret servant of your compulsion.

Share the kill later, by all means. But if you want to get rich, trust your judgement when it calls – and leave those whose job it is to manage your business to pick up the pieces. They can have the scraggy bits.

But the heart and liver are yours.

62

ON PERSISTENCE

You will find in the pages of many so-called 'self-improve-ment' books written by quacks (those who have never done something themselves but feel justified in pontificating about it to others) a great deal of drivel concerning the impor-tance of persistence. In such books, this word is spelt with a capital 'P' and treated as an object of idolatry and reverence.

Fortunately, this not a 'self-improvement' book. I do not believe anyone can be 'improved' by buying and reading a book. They can only be 'improved', if that is the word, by their own actions.

Persistence is important, vital even, and requires a concerted effort of will and stamina to maintain. But it is not an *end in itself*. Nor is stubbornness persistence. Stubbornness implies you intend to persist despite plentiful evidence that you are reinforcing failure. A stubborn person fears to be shown that he or she is wrong. A persistent person is convinced that he or she has been right all along; that the proof lies just around the corner.

'Never give in' is a useful catch phrase, but do not take it too literally. We must all surrender at some time – to love, or desire, or death. You will be forced into the last, and a fool if you never surrender to the first. But never give in *easily*. If you can, attempt one step further along the narrow road than appears sensible before calling a halt to regroup and chart a new course.

Above all, avoid banging your head against the same piece of wall. The wall will not get any softer. Persistence is only a virtue in the getting of money when applied with intelligence, and with the humility to accept that your strategy may be flawed.

63

ON TENACITY

Tenacity is not persistence and has nothing to do with stubbornness. Instead, it is a potent weapon in the armoury of those few destined to become far richer than their neighbours. I will go further. Not only is it a weapon – it is a fuel. A fuel to sustain those who continue the long trek on the narrow road when others have decamped and built their modest homesteads in the safer plains of mediocrity.

Tenacity will sustain and encourage you; not just to persist, but to do so in a more adaptable way. A persistent fly batters itself against a pane until it dies. A tenacious lioness experiments with several hunting strategies in order to feed. Eventually, because of her tenacity, she will succeed.

No book or advisor can imbue you with tenacity. Off in the wings there are always the gentle siren voices of friends, parents and employers – of reasonable and sensible people, torn between concern for your welfare and the secret, unspoken fear that you may succeed. A harsh reading of such concerns, perhaps, but a true one.

You must choose. Life is comfortable enough in the West. There are the safety nets of social services and of government-subsidised medical care. Decent jobs at decent salaries and a decent retirement, all without the heart-stopping fear of bankruptcy, of years of risk amid fears of ignominious failure. Why do handstands on the rim of hell? Why punish yourself? Nobody else you know is doing it – why should you? Make everyone around you happier. Why not give in?

If you are merely a wannabe, then the siren voices will prevail, and they will be right to prevail. If you are a gonnabe, if you have true tenacity, they will not prevail. Like Odysseus you will stop your ears with wax or bind yourself to the mast. You will learn to walk your narrow, lonely road – and to hell with the siren voices.

64

ON SELF-BELIEF

Coupled with tenacity, self-belief lies at the core of the getting of money. Without self-belief, nothing can be accomplished. With it, nothing is impossible.

Persistence offers you a second or third bite at the cherry. Tenacity ensures that you will continue to search for alternative ways to succeed. Self-belief encourages you to stare down failure and naysayers while tenacity works its magic.

It has been well said that 'no one can make you feel inferior without your consent'. Self-belief reinforces this axiom and is a priceless asset. We may profess to detest arrogance, yet isn't it true that we secretly *admire* it a little, too? Even though arrogance is a poor, shabby thing compared to rooted self-belief – an imitation of the real thing.

Which is not to say that self-belief should be permitted to trample on doubt as arrogance is wont to do. Doubt is like pain: both are antennae – one attuned to fallibility, the other to malfunction. Far better to embrace our doubts; without them, there is only naked ego, the kind of certainty that leads to untrammelled arrogance, to cruelty, or worse.

If you will be guided by self-belief tempered by a generous dollop of doubt, whether or not you succeed on the narrow road, you will perhaps dislodge a pebble to ricochet down the very small mountain of your life. This, in turn, may well create an avalanche that others will stand in awe of.

While I doubt I shall be among those clapping, you will certainly receive sufficient applause to repay your efforts. In time, you may even grow to enjoy the process!

65

ON LEADING

Lead. Do not be led.

You have hired a talented group of employees at your start-up, many of whom are smarter than you. Great. But you are their leader.

If you sniff an opportunity, get them to consider it. If they equivocate, call a meeting and brainstorm. If they still won't get excited, take the project into your private office and begin it there. Do not leave such an opportunity within the company to be sabotaged, focus-grouped and committeed to death – which is almost certainly what will happen if, for whatever reason, your colleagues are not excited by it.

How do you become a leader? By not seeking all the glory (only the money!) your smarter employees earn. And by uncompromising, sustained effort. As Warren Bennis observed in *On Being A Leader*: 'Leaders learn by leading, and they learn best by leading in the face of obstacles.' Aye, they do.

Similarly, when you find yourself involved in serious negotiations with a great deal at stake, do not permit financial or legal advisors to call the shots. They love to do this, to prove they are worth their fees. But *they* will not live with the consequences of a deal. *You* will. If you do not approve of the way advisors are behaving in such negotiations, call a time out and tell them so, privately. If they continue with their agenda, fire them on the spot. The world is full of professional advisors.

Your employees and advisors are just that; employees and advisors. *You* are the owner. You must follow your instincts. You must learn on the job. You must lead.

66

ON PROTECTING YOUR PIECE OF THE PIE

Sooner or later, someone is going to try to steal your piece of the pie – if not the whole damned thing. This will not be unfair. You almost certainly set out to steal someone else's in the first place.

Here they come – a rival or a huge corporation sniffing around your kitchen. They like the smell of what you've been baking and have decided to bake something similar. Well done! (You must have been doing something right.)

You can fight them, of course. You may well *have* to fight them. If your competitor is smaller, try to buy them or outsmart them by poaching their best talent. If they won't budge, consider taking drastic action. Instigate a price war and smash them. If that won't work, you must learn to be friendly rivals and collude against others.

If your rival is a larger company determined to park their tanks on your lawn, then consider carefully the possibility of *selling* your company or product to them. Perhaps the greatest business error I ever made was instigating a costly war against a huge competitor who had made clear their intention of stealing my pie.

When a large competitor comes calling, the potential of your own company or product is likely approaching its peak market value. It may well be time to cash out. With the hefty price they will pay, you can begin again, purchase a fine mare and proceed further down the narrow road in majestic style.

Riding is always preferable to walking, just as cashing out a little early in the getting of money is preferable to all-out war with a better-resourced enemy.

67

ON GOING PUBLIC

There is no comparison between running a private company and a public company. (By definition you cannot 'own' a public company, although you can certainly control one, providing you are willing to put up with a great deal of scrutiny.)

What is it like, taking the company you created public? A nightmare, usually. Endless meetings with bankers and their ferret-faced lieutenants. Lawyers salivating like hyenas and droning incomprehensibly to each other. Mountains of paper. A thousand warnings about what you can and cannot say that day. Fear and loathing, greed, and the sickening roller-coaster of emotions while your inner demons are screaming: *Do it! Do it! Do it at any price!*

And what do you discover, when you have banked tens of millions of dollars in your personal bank account with perhaps hundreds of millions of dollars to come?

You discover that a young public company exists only to boost its share price. That the balance between investment and profit-taking, between growth and bottom line, has dissolved. That growth is the only deity you may worship. That medium- and long-term strategies are for wimps and amateurs, according to spotty-faced youths called 'analysts'. That you have no choices. That you must grow or die.

This is all I know about going public. From my perspective, public companies are not sane places and their share prices are not decided by sane people, even though one such company made me very rich. Perhaps it is different when a company has been public for decades. But the first years of any such enterprise, in my experience, are ones of gut-wrenching adjustment, soul-destroying workloads and barely concealed terror.

It's a high price to pay for those at the sharp end. But hey! If you want to be rich, sometimes you have to sup with the devil. And no one cares, least of all the 'analysts', how long or how short your spoon is.

68

ON THE TROJAN TRAP

What is this we see? A young entrepreneur working like a Trojan – hyped up on fast food and caffeine. Working 16-hour days. Stumbling out into the night for a stiff drink and a swift curry and returning to the office for a few hours' kip on the office-sofa, only to begin the cycle all over again.

We see the same young man or woman dragging themselves in on weekends, pale with exhaustion. Snappy. Quick to criticise. Too slow to delegate or praise others. Almost at the end of their tether and determined never to give in.

We see someone who has fallen into the Trojan Trap.

Dumb move. The work undertaken by your colleagues and employees is more important than your work. Your job is merely to lead, to point the way, unless there is no one but you in the enterprise. (In which case, you had best stop reading this and get straight back to work.)

Battering yourself into setting world records for stamina and effort can only be sustained so long. You may be young, fit and determined, but your body is a machine – a machine that requires sleep, good-quality fuel and the odd day off. This is advice that will fall on stony ground for the uninitiated, but that doesn't make it any less true. It is *undisciplined* to permit yourself to fall into the Trojan Trap.

Making time to sleep well, eat well and take an occasional walk in the park is not *slacking*, not a betrayal of the cause. It's just good sense. The getting of money is a marathon, not a sprint. Keeping mentally and physically fit is essential.

If you doubt me, take a good look at a map of the world. Do you see anywhere marked 'Troy'?

69

ON SACRED COWS

One problem for start-up entrepreneurs is the tendency to treat what you create as a surrogate child. It becomes your 'baby'. This can prove savagely counterproductive because the world is constantly evolving and you must evolve with it – or perish.

Let's imagine you have raised a herd of sacred cows inside a fortress. Barbarians are at the gate. Killing sacred cows is a horrible crime, even though your defenders are short of food. If the barbarians overrun the fortress, the sacred cows will die anyway. If you kill *some* of the cows for your defenders to eat, they may be able to turn back the barbarians. Ergo, you sacrifice one or two sacred cows.

Sacred cows have always been with us. Recently, for example, the growth of the Internet began to destroy the music industry. Millions of music lovers downloaded songs without paying for them and CD sales went into tailspin. Record companies watched billions of dollars sucked out of the market, crippling their share values.

These record companies (who grew fat for years by charging high prices for cheap bits of plastic) reacted foolishly. They were slow to begin devouring the sacred cow of the CD. What they wanted was for the pirating and the illegal downloading to stop – and that's where they concentrated their initial efforts. Fat chance. The barbarians were not about to quit any time soon. They never do.

What the record companies were faced with was nothing new, merely a kind of forced diversification, but it *is* difficult facing up to swiftly changing realities on the ground. Most of us would prefer for things to stay pretty much the same so that we can carry on making money in the same way. But things do *not* stay the same.

Repeat this each day: 'I am not in the business of pampering babies or protecting sacred cows, no matter how hard I worked to breed them. I am in the business of the getting of money.

There is only one sacred cow in this organisation. *Me!*'

70

ON THE NEED
TO DIVERSIFY

This suggestion is not designed for the initial phase of a start-up. In the early days, one must concentrate upon weaving a single basket designed for a particular egg. You should focus as if your life depended upon that egg. In a way, it does.

But once that something *is* working, it makes sense to explore other avenues for creating revenue. This does not necessarily entail creating completely new baskets early on – merely expanding the manner in which money can be made by your company. At a later date, you can consider diversification into unrelated markets.

It is astonishing how often young entrepreneurs forget the need to diversify revenue streams. The world is a big place. If you are lucky enough to make something work in a particular locality, the chances are that it can be made to work elsewhere. Others might pay you to show them how to *duplicate* your basket.

Two factors conspire to retard such expansion: language and workload. There are only so many hours in a day and perhaps you speak only one language. No matter. Once the first flush of a successful start-up is over, you would be wise to make a choice: remain where you are to ensure continued growth, or entrust that task to others while you take to the road to license or franchise your product or service.

The narrow road is just that. It's a road. You travel upon it or stagnate. It's a two-way road, too – some of the best ideas you will ever encounter (and emulate!) are out there, pretested and free for the taking, if only you will seek them out.

Diversify just as soon as you sensibly can without imperilling your golden egg. I suspect you will find that the new eggs pretty much take care of themselves!

71

ON EXCELLENCE

If, on my deathbed, I had only a short time to pass what wisdom I had accumulated about the getting of money to a son or daughter, it would be this:

- *Ownership Shall Be Half Of The Law*
- *Doing An Outstanding Job Shall Be The Other Half*

Why should it count? Why is it important to concentrate on the excellence of your product and the manner in which your company is run? Aren't you supposed to be concentrating on getting rich?

Yes you are, but by insisting that those you employ do an outstanding job, you are helping to guarantee that goal:

- Talent will flock to a company with a reputation for excellence.
- You will make fewer errors, because of the excellence of your management.
- A reputation for excellence will enhance the asset value of your business.
- It is more enjoyable to own a company dedicated to excellence – you will relish coming to work and

will spend more time focusing on doing an even
better job.

And there is a last benefit attached to excellence. Should your
company fail (as, to be honest, many first start-ups do), the
reputation of what was produced will endure while the failure
of the business itself will soon be forgotten. That reputation
will stand you in good stead as you gather the resources necessary to return to the fray.

Striving for excellence works, any way one looks at it.

72

ON BONUS
ARRANGEMENTS

S alaries for senior employees are decided by the market. Bonus arrangements are yours to make. Make them generous if you wish your managers to concentrate on improving margin and bottom-line profit while growing the business.

Consider a three-part system for senior managers: two bonuses to be paid annually and a third at the close of a bonus cycle of three to five years. The first is for individual performance; the second is for performance as a group – to encourage self-policing against slackers. The third is the big pay day – by staying the course and delivering consistent profits and growth over an agreed number of years, all managers in the bonus pool receive a substantial additional bonus. This encourages your managers to turn their back on short-termism and guards against poaching.

Management short-termism in the quest to meet bonus targets is a real threat. What comprises the threat and how should it be dealt with?

Any manager can make short-term profits by slashing reinvestment. As an owner, while profits are welcome, you also require sufficient reinvestment to grow the business so as to increase its asset value. By 'ring-fencing' reinvestment money in your internal accounts for growth, you encourage managers to concentrate on margin and profit from existing parts of the business while offering them the chance to take a degree of risk on new projects without threatening bonuses. This equation requires goodwill and patience on all sides; but it can be done, and it works.

Whatever bonus arrangements you adopt, try to involve all the managers concerned when devising them – people take more seriously what they had a hand in creating. And do not forget discretionary bonuses. In the event of outstanding performance (especially in difficult financial times), it makes sense to err on the side of generosity.

73

ON RIVALS

Western capitalism is only made bearable by competition. *Death to monopolies!*

Your rivals will keep you honest and inspire you to emulate their successes. They are a terrific source from which to poach talent and fun to meet with from time to time, to swap notes and tell lies to each other. An entrepreneur who loathes his rivals is usually a fool.

Bad-mouthing rivals is a sign of weakness. You should set an example among your troops, encouraging them to analyse a rival's strengths rather than sneering at their failings. No individual or company is the font of all wisdom.

Go out of your way to praise rivals publicly when you can. Often enough they deserve such praise and they are sure to learn about your comments sooner or later. (Secretly feeling sorry for a rival owner or senior manager because they do not own as much of their company as you do of yours is perfectly permissible.)

Make it a habit to meet informally with a rival's talent when you can. I have never known a single person in a rival organisation, however well paid or cosseted, who refused to meet with me for a quiet drink after work. In this way, I have discovered more about what my rivals are up to than they ever imagined. Then too, I have often been so impressed with an individual that I poached them to work for me later. No intelligence-gathering exercise is ever entirely wasted in business.

It would be strange indeed if one or two direct rivals in your chosen industry did not eventually become good friends. The narrow road is lonely enough and a fellow pilgrim or two will keep you company along the way.

74

ON MISFORTUNE

Who will give a hoot whether you made five dollars or 500 million dollars a hundred years from now? Nobody will because it is not a matter of any great importance. No tragedy or real misfortune was involved.

Breaking your neck is a misfortune. Losing someone you love is a tragedy. Failing to accumulate a fortune on the narrow road is *not* a misfortune, it's just a part of the game. As H. L. Mencken put it: 'The chief value of money lies in the fact that one lives in a world in which it is overestimated.'

Be wary about claiming to be unlucky. Donning the mask of misfortune for the amusement of those around you or to elicit sympathy is a perilous activity. You run the risk of the mask fitting a little too well. Or – and I have seen this happen – of becoming the mask.

Financial losses are temporary reverses. How many times can you 'pick yourself up, dust yourself down and start all over again' following a business reversal? Even a catastrophic one? For those intent on the getting of money, the answer must be: 'As many times as it takes.'

You cannot fix a broken neck or bring back a beloved child from the grave. But you can always repair your fortunes on the road to riches. Should financial misfortune occur (and it probably will at some point) recall Winston Churchill's maxim from his days in the political wilderness:

When going through hell, keep going.

75

ON TAKING STOCK

In the mad rush to cement your company's success and begin accumulating wealth, it is easy to forget the necessity of taking stock. While the monitoring and forecasting of cash must be done on a weekly basis in the early stages, a single day set aside to analyse your progress occasionally is prudent.

Such analysis should be prepared for carefully and might include an examination of your financial results compared with the same period in prior years, a review of actual performance against your annual budget, and an appraisal of the progress made generally within your market sector. This is best done with all partners and senior managers present.

If you can afford it, such meetings may be held externally, perhaps in the conference room of a local hotel – it adds to the seriousness of the process and helps to keep distractions at bay.

Prior to these collective gatherings, there is one tactic that can prove highly beneficial to you as an owner – encouraging senior managers and accountants to go over recent financial results with you *one on one* and *line by line*. You will learn more about your financial position and prospects from off-the-cuff remarks and opinions expressed in one-on-one discussions than in a dozen collective meetings.

It is unwise to make strategic decisions when taking stock, though. The human brain is a grand instrument, but it works best when given a little time to digest information.

76

ON MUST-DO DEALS

Never fall in love with a deal. A deal is just a deal. There will always be other deals and other opportunities.

No deal is a must-do deal.

If it is, you are at the mercy of the party sitting across the table and – trust me – they will know this perfectly well. In that case, your goose is cooked and your future will already be in their hands.

77

ON THE RIGHT TIME
TO SELL A BUSINESS

The best time to sell a business is when you don't have to. The worst time is when you have little choice.

Just as there are very few jobs-for-life for employees in the 21st century, so there are likely be a number of quite separate businesses for an entrepreneur on the road to riches. The right time to sell a business is when there is still substantial growth potential present; the 'blue sky' one reads about in corporate brochures.

Try not to leave such a sale too late – the price a business is likely to fetch in such circumstances will be hugely diminished. It takes courage to sell something you've created before it reaches its full potential, but it is the only way to ensure that you obtain the best price possible. Don't concern yourself too much with what comes after a successful sale. With the money you pocket, a thousand new doors will open.

Another right time to sell a business is when you're bored with it. This happens more often than one might think. If you have fallen out of love with a business, it becomes difficult to disguise your lack of passion and commitment. This lack of enthusiasm will leak out no matter how hard you attempt to hide it, and will infect those around you. Employees will find this hard to forgive and easy to emulate. You should sell such a business without further ado.

In general, inexperienced entrepreneurs hang on to the businesses they create for far too long. You are in the game of the getting of money, so don't forget to *collect* the money from time to time.

You do that by cashing in your chips occasionally.

78

ON CONSEQUENCES

Everybody, soon or late, sits down to
a banquet of consequences.
Robert Louis Stevenson

Is the following true or false? 'There is only so much pie in the world; if you take more than your fair share, then someone else is going to go without.'

The sophistry of modern economic theory concerning the growth of *absolute* wealth in the world is not entirely convincing as a counter-argument. Wealth remains relative. Had my grandmother lived to see what passes for 'poverty' in Britain today, she would have got down on her knees and worshipped modern capitalism.

Just imagine: electricity in every home! She would marvel, too, at the central heating, carpeted floors, hot water on demand, indoor lavatories, the profusion of clothes and shoes in closets. What she might have made of the appliances – televisions, washing machines, refrigerators, dishwashers, computers and mobile phones – I cannot imagine. Or the cars parked outside. Yet these are now commonplace in the homes of those we deem to live below the 'poverty' line.

How can I know what my grandmother might have thought about such matters? Because I grew up with her, quite happily, in a home which had none of the above.

Even so, can it be right for anyone to seek to take more pie than their neighbour? I would answer that it *is* right, because the creation of entrepreneurial pie has been shown to beget yet more in absolute terms. While we can apparently do little to ease the strains arising from *relative* poverty and wealth, matters have greatly improved in the West since the middle of the last century, even for the poorest among us.

Just as much evil has been done in the world with the best of intentions, so much good has resulted from the 'evils' of capitalism in a mixed economy. Few British children walk the streets today malnourished, which was certainly not the case three score years ago.

79

ON STATUS

We are all leaves on the tree of life – or pencils in the hand of God, if you prefer Mother Teresa to endosymbiosis. Billions of leaves have sprouted before you and billions will sprout when you are gone. We might wish nature had ordered things differently, but at least she has ordered matters so that we are able to comprehend our insignificance, both as a species and as individuals.

In business, much may be achieved by high status. Understanding that those so designated are themselves leaves on the tree can go a long way towards puncturing the bubble of supposed invulnerability that surrounds status like an aura.

Do not be overly impressed by status in the getting of money. It is often decrepit. Longstanding status will have brought with it a stiffening of joints rather than sinews, and a hardening of mental arteries, leaving only a residue of experience and cunning. Those determined to achieve status are almost always in a better position to acquire it than those attempting to defend it.

All living things attempt to dominate their environments, even trees. But any forester will tell you that hybrid trees are invariably more vigorous and hardy than their so-called pure-bred progenitors. As a determined entrepreneur, however young and underresourced, you *are* that hybrid!

Wealth, at least, can be counted and measured, while status is a chimera. As a form of rank lacking any objective measurement other than perception, it mimics the divine right of kings. You will remember, of course, that the rise and adoption of mercantile capitalism dealt a death blow to that particular 'right' long ago.

80

ON QUALIFIED ACCOUNTANTS

Hire the best-qualified accountant or finance director you can afford, even *before* you can afford them.

Bean counters are one thing; qualified accountants and finance directors are another. Books and records need to be kept, but there will *be* no books and records to keep if you stint on full-time expert financial advice.

Such people will fight tooth and nail to reduce costs. They will impress suppliers and banks and help extend your credit. They will constantly remind you of the perils of overexpansion. They will become a burden and a pest to you every working day. But they will also ensure that you *survive*, if that is at all possible.

You will *not* find yourself having to grovel to a bank to pay a tax bill you failed to prepare for. You will *not* discover a landlord's bailiff at your door with a warrant to turf you into the street. Instead, you will free yourself to concentrate on growing your company while that blighter of a finance director constantly scolds you.

You will greet the arrival of your first finance director and chief operating officer with open arms. Then you will come to loathe them. Then respect will creep into the equation. Then you will hand them huge bonuses (and do so gladly) as the company turns the corner into blesséd profitability.

And one day you will find yourself taking time off from counting ill-gotten gains to pontificate to some young entrepreneur who seeks your advice. 'Hire the best-qualified accountant or finance director you can afford, even *before* you can afford them!' you will drone, sagely – just as I am doing now.

Oh yes, you will!

81

ON MILKING THE COW

It seems simple. It's *your* company; *you* created it and therefore it's *your* money. But it isn't, you know. That's not how the law sees it, not how your creditors see it and not how the tax authorities see it.

A limited-liability company is a legal entity. In theory, it is immortal and has rights and duties just as you do. It cannot be used as a personal milk cow to drain at will. You can certainly milk it, but only within reason, only when there is enough milk, and only in certain ways. If you deviate from permitted methods of milking it, you can find yourself in a heap of trouble rather quickly.

All money you take from your company must be paid as salary, a bonus, a dividend or the equivalent – and all such payments must be declared. This is the thing to keep in the forefront of your mind. Forcing your company into loaning you money personally is not a good idea – a red flag will go up in the local taxman's office. And 'benefits in kind' supplied by the company to you, to your friends or to your family will raise yet another flag.

The company's profits are the company's money. Despite being sole shareholder, if you take money out of the enterprise and do not declare it as salary, a bonus or a dividend, you can be accused of *stealing from your own company*, not to mention stealing from the taxman. It sounds bizarre, but it's true.

How to sum all this up? If your company can afford to pay you money, that's fine, just as long as you declare that it has been paid and are ready to cough up the tax on that payment. If you find other ways of squirrelling the company's money into your own pocket without reporting such a movement, you are almost certainly milking the cow in a way that is not permitted.

Now do you understand the need to hire the best-qualified accountant you can afford?

82

ON DRAGON CAGES

All, all of a piece throughout;
Thy chase had a beast in view;
Thy wars brought nothing about;
Thy lovers were all untrue.
John Dryden, *The Secular Masque*

The chase down the narrow road to riches is a long one. What has worked before may not work a second time. To focus only on Dryden's 'beast in view', on the tiny dragon one has just slain, is to miss the point. Time to move on.

You are not in the business of slaying dragons, though you may well be forced to do so occasionally. You are in the business of becoming as rich as you can, just as swiftly as you can.

When you have been lucky enough to make a little money, look carefully about you. Have you entered a dragon cage? Did you enjoy slaying that last dragon so much you are tempted to stay and slay more? Is that wise?

Most importantly, is this cage, this sector, this company you have created, the right environment for your next assault – can you really get rich in this place? Far, far too often, entrepreneurs sworn to the getting of money are lured into a dragon cage and come to believe it is their destiny to slay dragons. Perhaps it is.

But perhaps it would have made more sense to sell that first or second successful small enterprise, take the capital, and proceed further down the narrow road to a sign that reads: 'The Real Money Is Here!'

83

ON BUYING PRIVATE YACHTS, AEROPLANES, ETCETERA

D^{on't.}

If it flies, floats or fornicates, rent it. It's much cheaper in the long run.

84
ON CHEATING THE TAXMAN

Not worth considering, in my view. Taxes are an abomination, granted, but you are not in a position to muster the army necessary to counter that at the disposal of the taxman: bailiffs, the police, the fraud squad, the courts and all the rest.

One of the most important hires you will ever make, once you have earned a little money, is your *personal* financial advisor. This individual should work for *you*, not for your company. As soon as you have enough money, they should work for you full time. For many entrepreneurs they may become the nearest thing to a 'partner' you will ever have.

Finding ways for you to pay the least tax permissible is a personal financial advisor's job. It's simply not worth all the time and effort I have seen expended by certain entrepreneurs to concoct new wheezes and shadowy schemes for 'avoiding' taxes. Surely that time would have been far better spent making more money?

One can always make more money. The world is full of the stuff. But it is difficult to do so from the confines of a prison cell.

As an aside, I would add that if government was truly interested in extracting the maximum money from the rich (as opposed to posturing to the poor and middle-classes who vote for them), a flat 15 per cent tax on all income – of whatever type – would do the trick. Regrettably, such a policy would not only result in a massive increase in tax revenues, it would also lead to the loss of employment for many thousands of civil servants and financial advisors.

Heaven forfend!

85

ON BEING RIGHT...
OR WRONG

Being right or wrong is immaterial on the narrow road. The desire to be proven right in an apparently mad quest to become richer than one's neighbour may act as a spur. However, it may also become an impediment – especially in the event that being 'right' encompasses the success of a cherished idea or project.

All that matters is that one *becomes* rich. The means of achieving that goal – within the law – are neither here nor there.

'If it's a good idea, do it. It's far easier to apologise than it is to get permission.'
USNR Rear-Admiral Grace Murray Hopper

'Perhaps it is better to be irresponsible and right than to be responsible and wrong.'
Sir Winston Churchill

'Success has a thousand fathers. Failure is always an orphan.'
Anonymous (but claimed by many)

86

ON THE UNFAIRNESS
OF IT ALL

You there, sir! You sitting on a park bench with this book in your hand, shaking your head, because it's all too nasty to take in. Nasty? You have absolutely no idea how nasty it is and how nasty it is going to get.

If you can't take the heat, leave the kitchen. Take a hike. There are some of us here trying to make a sodding great fortune.

I suppose you'll be blubbering next about the starving children of Ethiopia. If you wish to save the starving children of Ethiopia then **do something useful with your life and get out there and save them**. Or better still, leave Ethiopia to its own devices. More damage has been done by do-gooders 'saving people' in Africa and elsewhere than famine ever wrought. Most of our aid only goes to prop up tyrants and dictators.

Or why not make a sodding great fortune yourself and then give it to them?

But get it into your head that the getting of money, of serious money, is not for the faint-hearted. It's sink or swim. Shit or bust. And we take no prisoners in this book because life takes no prisoners. Nobody gets out of here alive.

The best kind of fairness is the kind that makes money – lots of money. Then you can decide to do with it what you wish.

Giving it all away is a terrific option. But the Good Samaritan wasn't only a good man. He was a rich man, too.

Think on that, sir.

87

ON FAILURE

Things are not looking good. Your business plan was over-optimistic or the customers never arrived. You are up to your neck in financial trouble and worried sick about what to do next. What steps should you take?

- Keep things in perspective. This is not life or death; it's only money.
- Step back for a moment. Is the business failing because of lack of capital or would pouring more money in merely be throwing good after bad? Be ruthless in assessment. Try to examine your business as an outsider would.
- Could your business succeed as a tiger of a different stripe? Are there changes that might tip the balance from failure to success? If there is anyone with business savvy in the world you know and trust, now is the time to seek their advice.
- Do not trade illegally by continuing to order goods and services your cashflow forecasts suggest you are unlikely to be able to pay for. Such activity can interfere with your comeback. Seek the professional services of a receiver.

- Be straight with suppliers. You are about to become an irritating blip on their annual accounts – a bad debt. Do not compound your sin by making promises you cannot keep; you may require their goodwill when the dust has settled.
- Ensure staff get paid. Your suppliers factored in a bad-debt percentage in their budget. The young lad you employed has nothing factored in. He expects to be paid. He *needs* to be paid. He should be paid.

Closing down a business is a miserable affair. Shoulder the responsibility squarely. Get it done as fairly and responsibly as you can. And remember, there will be other opportunities later. You'll be back.

To paraphrase Oscar Wilde, experience is only the name we give to our failures.

88

ON SUCCESS

I bought your book and used it to find the narrow road. I still have it here, years later, tattered, full of underlinings and scrawled notes in the margins.

I have succeeded in becoming richer than my neighbour.

Thank you. Now what?

* * *

Well done, well done!

I will probably be dead by the time you come to this juncture. My posthumous advice is to cut that tiger loose from your ankle and begin giving your money away right now. (You might find that almost as hard as it was to make it.)

It was all just a silly game, wasn't it? Good fun, though.

Don't forget to help other young entrepreneurs when you can. But don't tell them what you found at the end of the road.

No need to spoil the surprise!

APPENDIX 1
WEALTH CALCULATED BY CASH-IN-HAND OR QUICKLY REALISABLE ASSETS

How rich is rich in the first decade of the 21st century? The following table is based on tax-paid cash-in-hand or assets which can be swiftly reduced to cash – publicly traded stocks and shares, bank drafts, gold, etc. It takes no account of assets that take time to realise without incurring loss in a 'fire sale' – your home, property, land, shares held in private companies, pension funds or fixed bonds. It also assumes you have relatively low debt and live in a Western democracy.

£50,000 to £199,000	The comfortable poor
£200,000 to £499,000	The comfortably off
£500,000 to £999,000	The comfortably wealthy
£1 million to £5 million	The lesser rich
£6 million to £15 million	The comfortably rich
£16 million to £35 million	The rich
£36 million to £49 million	The seriously rich
£50 million to £100 million	The truly rich
Over £100 million	The filthy rich and the super rich

Note: There are few people in the world who could put their hands on £100 million in cash in a week or even a month, no matter what they are worth. Such people have too much respect for money to leave that kind of change floating around in quick-release assets or cash. In addition, the reduction of any asset to cash very often leads to the imposition of capital gains tax – the equivalent of the Black Death to the rich.

APPENDIX 2
WEALTH CALCULATED BY TOTAL ASSETS (TRUE NET WORTH)

The true net worth of a person (as opposed to their quickly realisable assets) is difficult to estimate for a variety of reasons. Partly because of capital gains and other levies. Partly because death leads to death duties. Partly because of planned inheritance schemes and donations to trusts and charities.

Few rich people ever know their true net worth – the value of some of their major assets being difficult to estimate prior to a sale, and such sales often only occurring after the individual's death.

This table, then, is concerned with *estimated* total net worth, assuming that you are not about to die, that you are prepared to take time to cash out such assets and, again, that you have relatively low debt and live in a Western democracy.

£1 million to £2 million	The comfortable poor
£3 million to £4 million	The comfortably off
£5 million to £15 million	The comfortably wealthy
£16 million to £39 million	The lesser rich
£40 million to £74 million	The comfortably rich
£75 million to £99 million	The rich
£100 million to £199 million	The seriously rich.
£200 million to £399 million	The truly rich.
£400 million to £999 million	The filthy rich.
Over £1 billion	The super rich.

Note: The importance of taxation upon assets in such a table cannot be underestimated. In certain circumstances the true net worth of an individual or family might be reduced by as much as half in the event of death if little or no tax planning has been undertaken.

INDEX